James S Sensenig, N.D.

Straight Answers About Homosexuality For Straight Readers

the text of this book is printed
on 100% recycled paper

Straight Answers About Homosexuality For Straight Readers

David Loovis

BARNES & NOBLE BOOKS

A DIVISION OF HARPER & ROW, PUBLISHERS

New York, Hagerstown, San Francisco, London

A hardcover edition of this book is published by Prentice-Hall, Inc. It is here reprinted by arrangement.

First BARNES & NOBLE BOOKS edition published 1978

ISBN: 0-06-464022-1

78   79   80   81   82   10   9   8   7   6   5   4   3   2   1

Other Books by David Loovis

TRY FOR ELEGANCE
THE LAST OF THE SOUTHERN WINDS
GAY SPIRIT: A GUIDE TO BECOMING A SENSUOUS HOMOSEXUAL

For Peter, Alan, and The Boatslip

Contents

Straight Answers About Homosexuality For Straight Readers

Your "Cloud of Unknowing"

You were enjoying the party, and ready to edge toward the hors d'oeuvre table. Above the chatter, you heard someone remark clearly: "I'm gay." Others must have heard it; no one seemed to mind. Your stomach muscles clenched.

You've felt that spasm a lot lately. Homosexuality is everywhere—as a topic of casual conversation, as a fit subject for printed and televised daily news, as an off-hand trait of characters in TV situation comedies, or as a major trait of sympathetically portrayed heroes in books and in the movies and on the stage.

As if that weren't enough, it seems a relative of yours whom you thought you knew, a friend you used to like, a business associate with peculiar gall—all have gone so far as to declare themselves publicly as homosexuals or "come out of the closet," as they so quaintly phrase it.

Irksome. Even people you trust betray a cavalier attitude. If you are told one more time that others must be allowed to "do their own thing," you may throw up. A cloud hangs over the matter and over you. Your entire moral education is challenged.

You've been to the library; they have open shelves full of the stuff. But the doctoral dissertations confuse you, and the popular material is worse. Labeled "Gay Lib"—you found books and periodicals so blunt and biased your head swims.

You've tuned in to TV panel discussions about it. But the panelists look uncomfortable under the hot lights, nervous in front of the camera-eye and self-conscious concerning the things they discuss; the whole event appears specious to you. And the panelists mumble or interrupt or override one another. Even if you concentrate, it's impossible to follow an unfouled line of reasoning or argument.

You are not a person to avoid reality. Since homosexuality is ubiquitous, and it provokes in you such a troubling reaction, you will continue to probe. You have never been small-minded, superstitious or afraid. . . .

Straight Answers About Homosexuality for Straight Readers speaks to your need; it will pierce and dispel your cloud of unknowing. In this book, I have made an effort to afford you a purchase on the subject that will not defy you. Further, the narrative is in question and answer form, and in the person of the *questioner*, I believe you will find ample articulation of your anxieties about homosexuality, as well as an interlocutor who requires facts as to the exact nature of homosexuality. I am primarily homosexual, of course; it seems to me you cannot get an illuminating interpretation of the matter from someone who is not, or from someone who "fudges" it by omitting to indicate his primary sexual preference. *Straight Answers* is aimed at your edification.

But I have had a second and, in my mind, equally important purpose in writing this book. In addition to information, I want to provide you in the course of your reading with a specific personal benefit.

What is that benefit?

An evocation in you of a homosexual sensibility.

Oh, no! I can hear your outcry! It must seem to you like the offer of a third ear on top of your head. Who needs it? What can you do with such a thing? I say to you that as curious as it may sound, the evocation in you of this "sensibility" will give you a firmer grasp on homosexuality than can ever be achieved by someone who is merely informed about it. An evocation in you of this sensibility will equip you with everything you've always wanted to *truly know* about the subject. I am talking about the kind of insight that is going to cure you of those muscle-spasms.

2

When I term it "your homosexual sensibility," do I have in mind that you must rush out and engage in homosexual sex?

Of course not. But I will ask you to seriously consider in reference to yourself *a fact of human nature which is becoming increasingly apparent and widely accepted:* everyone is potentially both heterosexual *and* homosexual. The great mystics and philosophers have told us so for centuries, seconded in recent decades by the great psychologists. *Repressed* in you, despised probably, a junkyard object that the veto of social conditioning has caused it to be—the homosexual sensibility exists. It does in everyone.

But hadn't that sensibility, *if* indeed it is a component part of your nature, better remain repressed—lost, with good reason?

No. This so-called "lost" factor in you *with its emphasis on love and vulnerability,* has a function in relation to your heterosexual sensibility. In brief, it is the ameliorating force in you against the pressure of a demanding heterosexual existence; it is the natural inner compensation for excess of heterosexual *striving for money and prestige* that drops men in their tracks at fifty and renders women intractable at forty—your homosexual sensibility is the necessary opposite in you that strikes the balance!

Consciously evoked and understood, your homosexual sensibility will return to you a fount of psychic energy—which was wasted in its repression.

You will be put in command of new sources of joy: a delight in the body, always part of the homosexual sensibility; a more profound appreciation of all forms of art, through which, these days especially, that sensibility suffuses its aura. You will experience a renewed quality of child-likeness and the ability to "play," ever concomitants of that sensibility.

In the conscious evocation of your homosexual sensibility, you will discover a point-of-identification with those individuals (relatives, friends, business associates) who've integrated homosexuality into their public lives. That identification will give you a more acute awareness and a sharper comprehension of our modern world.

So—come with me through *Straight Answers*. Let us consider the subject in the mood of friendly adversaries, bound to reach detente. In the person of the answerer-advocate, it will be my goal to dispel your cloud of unknowing about

3

homosexuality—and replace it with bright day.

I have drawn the material in this book from my own homosexual experience, from my current involvement with the gay lib movement, and from my knowledge of most of the recently published, pertinent books and periodicals, gay and otherwise, including:

After You're Out, edited by Karla Jay and Allen Young
Book of Men, A, edited by Ross Firestone
Church and the Homosexual, The, by Father John J. McNeill
Consenting Adults, a novel, by Laura Z. Hobson
Everything You Always Wanted to Know about Sex, by Dr. David Rubin
Familiar Faces, Hidden Lives, by Howard Brown
Front Runner, a novel, by Patricia Nell Warren
Gay American History, by Jonathon Katz
Gay Insider USA, The, by John Francis Hunter
Gay Men Speak, by Ronald Lee with Frank Melleno and Robert Mullis
Gay Mystique, The, by Peter Fisher
Gay Power, by Barry Cunningham
Gay Sex Techniques, by Walter Norris
Heterosexual, by Nancy Davis and Jeff Young
Homosexual, by Dennis Altman
"Homosexual Imagination, The," special edition of the magazine *College English,* November 1974
Homosexuality and Counseling, by Clinton R. Jones
Homosexual Matrix, The, by C. A. Tripp
Homosexual Handbook, The, by Angelo d'Arcangelo
I Have More Fun with You Than Anybody, by Lige Clark and Jack Nichols
Joy of Gay Sex, The, by Dr. Charles Silverstein and Edmund White
Lord Is My Shepherd and He Knows I'm Gay, The, by Rev. Troy Perry
Lord Won't Mind, The, a novel, by Gordon Merrick
Making Love, by Michael Kearns
Male Homosexuals, by Martin S. Weinberg and Colin J. Williams
Men's Liberation, by Jack Nichols
On Being Different, by Merle Miller
Out of the Closets, edited by Karla Jay and Allen Young
"Parents of Gays," a pamphlet, copyright by Betty Fairchild
Phallos, by Thorkil Vanggaard
Pleasure Bond, The, by William H. Masters and Virginia E. Johnson
Pumping Iron, by Charles Gaines and George Butler

Rights of Gay People, The, by E. Charrington Boggan, Marilyn
   G. Haft, Charles Lister, and John P. Rupp
Roommates Can't Always Be Lovers, by Lige Clark and Jack
   Nichols
Same Sex, The, edited by Ralph W. Weltge
Sensuous Man, The, by M
Sensuous Woman, The, by J
Sex and Human Life, by Eric T. Pengelley
Sexual Outlaw, The, by John Rechy
Straight/White/Male, edited by Glenn R. Bucher
"Twenty Questions about Homosexuality," a pamphlet, by the
   Gay Activists Alliance
"Unbecoming Men," a pamphlet, by Mike Bradley, Lonnie
   Danchik, Marty Fager, and Tom Wodetzki
"Universities and the Gay Experience, The," a pamphlet,
   sponsored by the Gay Academic Union

In addition, I've briefed myself on the following gay
magazines: *Mandate, Blue-Boy, Michael's Thing, In Touch,
Christopher Street, David, Play-Guy.* Also, to be up-to-date, I
have read most issues of gay-oriented newspapers over the
period of a year, particularly the established *Los Angeles
Advocate* and the up-and-coming *Esplanade.*

Straight Answers, deals almost exclusively with male
homosexuality. I regard lesbianism with respect, and I shall
leave you to interpretations of it by specialized writers in the
field, probably women.

By "Straight" answers, I don't mean simple answers; there
aren't any. Homosexuality is a complex subject, and answers
to questions about it may be complicated. Further, my manner of presentation to you will involve occasional over-lapping
of statements, and some repetition of difficult points in an
effort to be clear. We are after the facts and emotional truths
of the matter. I shall state the facts honestly, with decorum.
The emotional truths are best served, I feel, by a description
of the contradictions, paradoxes and conundrums of
homosexuality as the homosexual himself experiences them.
As you begin to see life through his eyes, you will evolve your
homosexual sensibility.

The questions posed in *Straight Answers* are your questions, rendered acerbically now and then as a reflection of
your feeling.

The answers given in *Straight Answers* are my answers,
based on the facts about homosexuality as I perceive those

5

facts, with some leavening of laughter. Each answer I give is also a human interpretation or conjecture, a confession or a belief.

Chapter 1

The Dirty, Tough Questions

What is meant by "dirty, tough questions"?

These are questions asked by certain straight people who are, first, *unfamiliar* with homosexuality except for hearing derogatory rumors about the acquaintance of an acquaintance, except for seeing a homosexual on TV or in a movie who with frequency turns out to be the bad guy. Two, these questions are asked by straight people when they come upon evidence of homosexuality *unexpectedly:* a "queer" with long hair walks into a straight luncheonette, or a straight couple accidentally walks into a gay bar or across a gay beach. Three, these questions are asked by people *having a hard time suppressing curiosity* about homosexuality, also inner hostility toward themselves for that curiosity. From all three, such questions are not questions, but taunts and vilifications.

In short, red-neck questions?

Yes, but worth answering with as much care *for the questioner* as for the content of his questions.

Why would such a questioner be worth caring about?

Because at one time or another, such questions occur to everybody, even gay people: I have seen an angry gay person scream out "Faggot!" at another person no more and no less gay than himself. The dirty, tough questions aren't posed to elicit answers, but there *are* answers. I have seen a dirty, tough questioner's wrath turned aside with a quiet straight answer. I have even seen him change into his opposite—into someone genuinely concerned about people who are homosexual—and occasionally I have seen such a person at the tip end of an argument willing to admit his own potential homosexual urge, whether or not he has ever acted upon it. These dirty, tough questions are not limited to the shouted epithets of a gang of laborers in the back of a pickup truck.

Don't queers molest children?

Children are molested by pedophiliacs, and most pedophiliacs are not homosexual (*Gay Activist Political Primer*, Question 17). Gays have borne the cruel stigma of child molesters for years. Most molested children are girls, and their molesters are heterosexual (same source). When a male child is molested, the event is sensationalized, and homosexuals are, as usual, fair game. Every gay person is at fault for merely existing, if you believe the implication of the newspaper accounts.

The devil can quote scripture. Why should your answers, despite their sources, be accepted?

A key question that is going to save us time if I answer it here once and for all. *Straight Answers* would not be necessary if a large body of incontrovertible knowledge about homosexuality existed. It does not. There is no such body of knowledge about heterosexuality. There are official homosexual "reports": part of the Kinsey Report; the Wolfenden Report in England; the National Institute of Mental Health Report, and others—all of which concur in the need for more detailed studies. What does exist in the minds of many is a store of hideous prejudice and superstition about homosexuality. *Straight Answers* is an attempt to dissolve the unreality of such thinking, and replace it with the facts about homosexuality, and such other *intimate emotional truths* of homosexuality as have been learned by me. That this book is *my interpretation* of the subject has been noted.

You mean it boils down to your say-so against mine?

Yes. But I shall give your say-so a hearing. No matter how tough or dirty your question may be, I'll try to summon up a reasonable and informed answer. I ask you to give my say-so a hearing in return. By that mutual exchange, perhaps we can get a dialogue going in which some part of the truth may be approximated.

Don't queers want to put the make on every straight guy they meet?

No, gay people do not. There are gay people who prefer sex with an ostensibly straight male, but they are roughly equivalent to heterosexual men who prefer sex with lesbians. Some gays are attracted to "butchy" boys, who, in fact, once they are separated from their buddies, thoroughly enjoy fellatio, and accept money so as to justify their participation to themselves. Your question here is understandable, but it is on the order of thinking done by a woman who believes every man in the room is after her.

Aren't queers ravening sexualists?

No, but the idea is prevalent with a venerable history: I first got this notion from pictures on Greek vases—satyrs prancing with caricatured gigantic erections. Or those stories of elves cavorting in certain woodland dells presumed to be haunted, and only safe for regular folk to enter when the first rays of the sun peeked over the mountaintop. All that berry-juice drinking and dancing wildly and those orgies—Dionysius unbound! I'm sorry, but the reality is somewhat less romantic. What is true is that at bar closing time in town or at the popular resorts, you do find gay people exploring a nearby relatively unlighted place for a partner who up until that hour has been as unlucky as himself in making a contact.

How is it, then, that queers are known for their over-preoccupation with sex?

Since homosexuality is considered unusual, and since a lot of what you hear or read about gay people concerns their "fleshly passions," word has gotten about that the only thing gay people think of is their next orgasm. I assure you gay people, like everybody else, have job needs to fulfill, living quarters to keep clean, family obligations in requirement of satisfaction, and certain purely social busywork to do. Like straight people, most gay people look forward to weekends for making love. And as straight people employed in an office during the week are prone to ogle a pretty secretary, so gay people in the same office are, during the week, prone to ogle a pretty mail boy. Would you say that both oglers are sex-obsessed, neither is, or just the gay person?

But why do there seem to be strong erotic "vibes" around homosexuals?

Could be you read them in, and/or you're interested. But you do win a "point" for that observation; there is truth to it. Also, your observation is evidence of your nascent homosexual sensibility. It is something gay people of any age try never to lose: that impression, however slight, of active sensuality. In the broadest possible sense, love and sex remain live currents for most gay people as long as they're still breathing.

Shouldn't that sort of thing be outgrown?

Outgrown, you say—by whom? Certainly, the incredible sale of how-to-do-it sex manuals isn't for the instruction of homosexuals. The majority of pure porn is straight. It would seem that largely a heterosexual population has forgotten which end is up and wants to have its recollection refreshed. It is all very well to say that that sort of thing should be outgrown, but evidently a lot of people don't believe in out-growing it, and in fact, want to be good at arousing another's concupiscence. And that large majority is heterosexual. Why single out a homosexual for immature devotion to sex when his straight brothers and sisters are right in there beside him? Or is there some slight resentment on your part that sensual-ity sustains so naturally in a gay person?

Does it?

I think it does, but alas, not always by virtue of his choosing. A gay person is as charged with psychic energy as a straight person, but as a gay person, he is discriminated against in the commercial adversary arena. Denied in part his legitimate place in the competitive world—or denying it to himself for conflicts of oppression he feels unfair and unable to deal with—the unchanneled psychic energy of a gay person may well be invested in love and sex.

So gay people *are* ravening sensualists?

No. They are observably interested in their sexual orienta-tion, true. They are needful of love as they are for air, true. And some are past masters at sex, true. But none of that indicates a ravening sensuality.

Isn't your real, secret aim in this book to proselytize homosexual sex, just like every queer tries to do?

No, sorry. What you do in bed doesn't concern me. What does, in this book, is evoking out of yourself your repressed homosexual *sensibility*, as the best method of comprehending homosexuality in general. Also, in *Straight Answers*, I hope you will come to see life as a gay person sees it, and share in some of the illuminations of his viewpoint.

11

What about *his* learning from *me*?

That's not the issue here. I am trying to show you two things: a homosexual sensibility exists in you, and that its emphasis on love and vulnerability can benefit you as a power-driven, uptight heterosexual.

What about *his* need for more of my power-drive?

Gay people have *not* eschewed power willingly; relieve them of the many kinds of oppression they suffer and let them into the commercial adversary arena on all levels, and you will see what efficacious fighters they can be, how quickly they pick up on procedure. On the other hand, many heterosexuals have willingly eschewed love and sex for the fulfillments of the power game, at the price of their psychic well-being; a realization that usually comes too late.

What do you mean, too late?

I mean, without some stimulant to love, a straight power-game player in mid-life is prone (if I read Jung correctly), to a diminution of vitality, of flexibility, and of human kindness. Resulting in premature rigidity, crustiness, stereotypy, fanatical one-sidedness, obstinacy, pedantry, or else resignation, weariness, sloppiness, irresponsibility, and finally a childish ramollissement, with a tendency to alcohol.

The *extremes* that homosexuals go to stand in the path of any appreciation or adaptation by me of a homosexual sensibility—how do you account for the horror of what transsexuals do to their bodies?

Transsexuality is a distinct and separate phenomenon from homosexuality. It is not all *one*. And in defense of transsexuals—it is *not* a matter of what they "do" to their bodies: as if the psychiatric examination, the hormonal treatment, and the sex-change operation were refined methods of self-destruction!

A transsexual believes that "she" has liberated in actuality a woman's mind and sex drive that were imprisoned always in her previously male body. The sex-change operation is no casual affair: It is preceded by years of self-questioning and months of formal psychiatric examination—to determine whether or not the idea of a "woman's brain in a man's body" is a temporary obsession or a genuine conviction. And the facts about living as a transsexual (especially in America) are made clear to "her." Then, usually, the hormonal treatments are begun. If, after all of that, "she" still feels as "she" did, legal precedents (for permission of any serious operation) are fulfilled and the sex-change operation is performed. The male genitals are removed, and a vagina is constructed of implanted tissue. The respectable Johns Hopkins Hospital maintains a staff who perform such operations.

I myself do not equate my homosexuality with a woman's mind and sex drive, nor can I conceive of myself having the courage of such an irreversible commitment under any circumstances. But I respect those who do.

What about the nonsensical things transvestites do to themselves?

Transvestites are notoriously heterosexual, mascara notwithstanding. You characterize them as "nonsensical." They make sense to themselves, I assure you. Certain males feel safe and happy dressed as women. Haven't you noticed, by the way, how many *women* enjoy wearing pants, boyish shirts, even suits; Saks Fifth Avenue and Brooks Brothers, just to cite two stores, have entire departments where they hawk these mannish items. You don't single out their patrons for condemnation. In the bedroom, the heterosexual practice of a husband borrowing his wife's undergarments (so that the wife wears the pants, as it were) is not that unusual. Transvestitism is an expanded form of similar fetishism, and has little to do with homosexuality.

I looked in on a convention of transvestites, and besides seeming quiet and kind people (often escorting wives), I was amused by their frequent references to "brother": the life that brother lived, how he worked, thought, etc. I needed a moment before I realized that brother was the appellation transvestites use in discussing themselves in everyday guise, a thing they don't lose sight of.

Another type of male (who may or may not be homosexual) dresses in women's clothes. He wears a little print sundress, say, along with boots and a full beard. This is called cross-dressing. The point of it is to confound old ideas of what males and females "should" be, or what they "should" behave like or, indeed, what they "should" wear. If you haven't seen a cross-dresser striding down the street, you have missed a funny parody of mores. His action is not nonsensical either, but has a gay or woman's lib motive behind it.

Drag queens are extreme; aren't they homosexual?

Yes. In preparing *Straight Answers*, I thought it might be necessary to include a glossary of "gay" terms, but I can see from your ready use of the vernacular that that won't be required.

Drag queens! What a burden of merde they have endured. Do you know that the gay lib movement has come to the conclusion, rightly I believe, that drag queens, as you call them, or female impressionists, as professionals are known, (or just little swishy queens without drag) are *the earliest gay lib heroes!* They had the good old American guts to appear as the people they felt they were! Plus an element of exaggeration and defiance. Forced to the wall over the issue of their homosexuality, they said to themselves and to the world—the hell with it, I am what I am! And dared to take Thoreau's advice, and to their own selves were true—unlike the rest of us gays who remained in our closets wearing striped ties.

I can understand how you might feel leery of gay flamboyance, that camping and swishing obviousness might offend, put you off from your consideration of the homosexual sensibility as a creative addition to your own personality. "If that's what it's all about," I can hear you saying, "who wants any part of it!"

That is part of it, at least it *was* part of it when the homosexual in society was an embattled individual who reacted viciously in response to the viciousness he encountered on every side. Sadly, he experienced viciousness even in his own heart, toward himself; deeply inculcated, long-standing. And that was the core reason for his "obviousness": a defense against his own self-hatred—and that concept of himself was *for once and truly* not his fault, but society's, as has now been revealed. No homosexual need act that way any longer.

If a gay does camp and swish, he does it out of momentary throwback to the old days, or out of humor, and the sense of irony and parody that is an ancient residue in the homosexual sensibility. And if he wears drag, or if you see a female impressionist on the stage "doing" his best Mae West—laugh, for God's sake, laugh with him. His is the minstrelsy of the saints; he has earned bitterly his cap and bells, and he wears them proudly! Let him do his little tricks for your amusement.

Don't queers fear women, if they don't actually hate them?

I don't fear or hate women; I've never met a gay person who does. A woman whose interest in gay people is a disguise for wanting to "change" gays into straight, or whose need for a dependent male is urgent sometimes seeks out the company of gays. A fag hag, when she's hooked one, turns around like a mother guppy and eats him psychologically, or, having forced herself on him, loudly proclaims he's using her. Such women are difficult people but their motives or activities wouldn't inspire fear or hate. On the contrary, the nurturing effect, especially of older women on young gay people, is well known. Tennessee Williams' recent *Memoirs* are replete with examples of his friendships with older women. Proust was in a constant state of infatuation with them. Or, to turn it around, would Ernest Hemingway have been the writer he was but for a certain Gertrude Stein, well-known lesbian?

What is homophobia?

It is a recently coined word meaning a profound, irrational, and active dislike of homosexuals.

How does it manifest itself?

The neck hairs of a homophobic male bristle at the idea, much less the presence, of a homosexual. Hemingway was known to·

break a wineglass when he sat near a known homosexual in a ship's dining room. When the subject of homosexuality arises in conversation, a homophobic woman will leave her company to see how dinner is coming on. More virulent homophobia leads townie kids in summer resorts to ambush homosexuals after dark, and causes otherwise sane police to take a poke at a gay person just for the hell of it. Subtle homophobia results in the impossibility of advertising in the straight media in detail for a book on a homosexual theme; results in housing or job discrimination, despite the homosexual's complete acceptability and competence. Not so subtle homophobia results in periodic harassing police raids on gay bars, baths, and beaches at the same moment that real crime is rampant in any given area; and to the calculated "entrapment" of homosexuals, who, until the plainclothes detective arrives on the scene, has committed no crime.

Homophobics have reportedly associated homosexuality with communism, vampirism, wan voices and weak constitutions, ribbon clerks, sharklike sexual appetites, seduction of children, Oscar Wilde's disgrace, with remittance checks and blackmail, bitch fights, circus hermaphrodites, devil worship, shiny loafers and satin pants and long cigarette holders, limp wrists, sadistic and anonymous murder, mental lassitude, physical enervation and job neglect. Homophobia, thy real name is superstition.

But weren't we taught homosexuality was just damned wrong?

Yes, most of us were taught that. Damned wrongly. We were, some of us, also taught to hate Jews and blacks and Italians and the Polish—anyone or anything that did not happen to be WASP and heterosexual.

But aren't homosexuals basically different from anyone else?

The answer is no, they are not different. The object of homosexual preference is a male, but the emotions a homosexual feels in love are exactly the same emotions that you feel in love. I admit that comes as a surprise sometimes: Since the object of gay sex and love is different, so must the mind of a gay person be different. Not true. This realization of absolute similarity is hard to bring home until your son or daughter or relative or friend or business associate confesses to you his/her homosexuality. "But you're just like me," is the usual reaction, followed by: "I never knew you were so different," followed by: "How could you deceive me!" Nobody deceived anybody, as you will discover ultimately; no basic difference exists, or ever existed, except in the "object of affections." Your relative or friend or business associate continues to share with you all the treasured emotional bonds that you had together in the first place.

But won't our relationship change, if I find out they're gay?

No, hardly at all. The relationship need not change, except to broaden, providing *you change your ideas* about homosexuality if those ideas stir in you a nameless rancor or, more usually, disgust. Whether or not the relationship changes, or you retain your conception of homosexuals as basically different, is up to *you*.

Why are homosexuals so difficult to tolerate, much less identify with?

Because they are the projected shadow-side of yourself. Gay people seem to offer a hook on which to hang everything that you—and the human race—consider inferior, or sinful and demonic, or sick and neurotic, or unadapted, or retarded, or incomplete *about yourself!* The conscious mind bundles up these negative qualities and represses them; they become unconscious but not lost—*these qualities are projected.* You then react unfavorably, to say the least, to what you think you see when a homosexual enters the room. He needn't open his mouth but you feel you know all about him. What you "know" is primarily your projected image.

Shouldn't that "shadow-side" better stay repressed?

People today are learning to reexamine, if they can, the contents of their unconscious: to face down the horrors that they fear reside there. What is dredged up is a lot of superstition in terms of blurred images of people and things. Homosexuality is one of the most firmly repressed of these unconscious contents, and as a complex it is loaded to boot with all sorts of other unpleasant associations. But this is the slime of the deep. Straight people are learning that there is nothing to fear from their potential homosexuality; they are learning to separate it from these other unpleasant associations and reexamine it for what it is—an inestimably important part of their psychic equipment, in ways that I've mentioned, and shall continue to delineate. They are beginning to realize that in crushing any trace in themselves of a homosexual sensibility, they have indeed thrown the baby out with the bathwater.

If I were inclined to do so, how could I cure my homophobia?

Try to picture some beloved near-relative or cherished friend or esteemed business associate whom you know or suspect of being homosexual and ask yourself if your homophobic ideas fit that person.

Or, with utter honesty—and we will come back to this subject in greater detail in Chapter 2—ask yourself if you haven't, at some time or other, felt an emotion of deep affection for someone of the same sex as you, which, if it had gone on unchecked, might have led to a homosexual relationship on your part. If the answer is yes, then you must know homosexual emotion is a *human emotion*—and with that realization at least gay people slip out of the "monster category" where your homophobia always placed them. If the answer is no, then I ask you to consider that there are 20 million homosexuals, and that they are not monsters but people, and I ask you to make an "imaginative leap" into their lives, and again, after this experiment, see if you can justify your homophobic projected images. I think you will find after a little *serious* examination that what you have are 20 million people who happen to be homosexual, different from you in their sexual tastes only, but people, after all. If you can accomplish that in yourself, you have made a start toward curing your homophobia.

Why should I hire a queer if I have a job opening in my company—especially if there's a straight guy available equally as qualified as the queer?

For God's sake don't hire the "queer" as you refer to him under those circumstances. You'd be unhappy, he'd be unhappy. If a straight guy is not available, however, or isn't as qualified for the job as the gay applicant—*don't* hire the "queer" anyway. Allow your homophobia to stand in the way of getting the job done well, and give up what profit might accrue to the job well done. I'm being sarcastic, of course. Employers are beginning to understand that homosexuality is not a contagious disease, that gay people make devoted workers if they are not harassed about their sexual adjustment, that there are many jobs they do as well as or better than their heterosexual counterparts, and that because they are not usually engaged in raising a family, gay workers have more psychic energy generally to bring to their job. Also (sarcastic again), a "token" queer on the payroll, like a "token" black, is good public relations. Businessmen are aware nowadays that there is a substantial block of homosexual purchasing power.

Won't a queer male or female teacher, especially in grade school, make a pass at my child, or attempt to proselytize homosexuality?

Let me answer you this way: Which of us, gay or straight, can't remember from our elementary or high school days that disciplinarian lady teacher who wore tweed suits and low-heeled shoes, no makeup, and tied her hair in a bun, who made us do more homework than the other teachers and who was inclined to dispense demerits freely. More likely than not, she could be observed after school being met by another lady who looked very like herself. And which of us has not memories of that idealistic, pipe-sucking loud-mouthed gym teacher who showered with the boys, towel-slapped backsides with the best of them—and went home to his bachelor apartment or his mother's house. And doesn't it come back to you that those two teachers were the most revered and honored in the whole school, that their pupils agreed they were tough but fair: that at graduation everyone wanted the signatures of those two teachers especially, in their memory books, and that you have remembered them vividly for years, and sometimes with tears. Do you really believe that those two figures from all our pasts weren't homosexual?! Christ, dear gay teachers eternally have been giving children the ideas and hopes and dreams for the children's lives which set the highest standards! Not only as individuals, but as citizens of this great nation. If you consider that as subversive proselytizing, I say the kids today could use more of it.

How can queers fool around with that queer stuff they're constantly spouting when there are buildings to be built and money to be made and dames to be laid in the straight world?

You get a "point" for that question. Gay people are sometimes overly self-absorbed with their own sexuality, and they do tend to insulate themselves by setting up their own communities here and there.

Like cancer in the body politic?

No, like oases in a desert of fear and superstition. I tell you it is a relief to me to go after working all day in the straight world to a gay bar for a cocktail—"I would drink for a space the unmingled wine"—and to groove on what I see and hear.

Up until recently, being homosexual and remaining *sane* was a full-time preoccupation. Pure survival in the straight world of business called for evasion, dissembling, and suppression of everything homosexual—a double life for gay people. If you knew you had something real and worthy to offer the straight world in the way of an aptitude, ability, or talent, no matter the field of work, as a gay person you had to do handstands emotionally if you were to be allowed to make your contribution, and to receive your rightful and earned compensation. Or, if you were living with your lover, when your parents, or his, came to visit you and what they called your "roommate," you had to be certain that there were *two obviously separate* beds in the apartment. And then, if they stayed for dinner, you had to have "dates," (gay girls or wise straight girls), who would come in and play the game. The unrelenting necessity of "appearances" was a full-time job. Small wonder in their "off-time" gay people immersed themselves in their gay life.

How can queers resist the obvious logic of nature that dictates a penis belongs in a vagina, not in somebody's mouth or in their anus?

As to the "logic of nature" of which you speak, let's turn to a book called *Sex and Human Life*, by Eric T. Pengelly: "Homosexual behavior is found in various forms almost throughout the animal kingdom," and "So far as mammals are concerned, it is safe to say that in all species that have been studied homosexual activity has been observed and is indeed common."

It would seem that animals, most subject to the "logic of nature," do not—with regularity—proceed logically. Neither, for that matter, do heterosexual men and women. Oral and anal penetration are almost always included now in books on the joy of sexual variations; in fact, encouraged—to break up old routines. Why, then, hold homosexuals to a "logic of nature" which others, with profit, have abandoned? Poor old "nature's logic"! The sun revolves around the earth, remember?

In Chapter 5, we'll discuss theories of the origin of homosexuality and whether or not sly old (not-so-logical) Mother Nature didn't have a birth control scheme up her sleeve when she invented homosexuals. Incidentally, domestic cows are quite gay when it suits them.

The Bible! What about the Bible? Those injunctions against queerness—won't those stand in the way of anybody developing a homosexual sensibility?

Ah, yes, the Bible. Before I answer your question directly, are you aware that St. Paul exhorted slaves to stay with their masters; that the old Testament forbade eating shrimp or women wearing scarlet apparel; that there are biblical passages *declaring women inferior to men*—that in Leviticus

18:22, He says: "You shall not lie with a male as with a woman; it is an abomination." God speaks only about male homosexuality and he speaks only to males about it. Small points, perhaps, but persuasive in a direction. . . .

In a book called *The Manufacture of Madness* by Thomas S. Szasz we are told, "The Church opposed homosexuality not only, or even primarily, because it was 'abnormal' or 'unnatural' but rather because it satisfied bodily lust and yielded bodily pleasure. This condemnation of homosexuality, says Rattray Taylor" (I am still quoting Szasz) "'was merely an aspect of the general condemnation of sexual pleasure and indeed of sexual activity *not directly necessary to insure the continuation of the race*. Even within marriage, sexual activity was severely restricted. . . .'"

So—you have your answer to those biblical injunctions. It is regrettable that such prohibitions have, until recently, influenced our contemporary criminal laws and social attitudes which regard homosexuality as a hybrid of crime and disease. Biblical prohibitions, by the way, influenced churchmen of medieval times to equate homosexuality with heresy or witchcraft, and a number of men and women were burned at the stake for it. I think you would agree that our problem today is not "continuing the race," but how to stop too-efficient breeding, especially among people who can't provide for the children they propagate. Biblical injunctions applied to another place and another time, and if you do not think so, throw away "the pill," retain your slaves, continue to derogate women and stop eating shrimp.

What do you think of David Rubin's chapter "Male Homosexuality" in his book *Everything You Always Wanted to Know About Sex . . .*?

A good question for this chapter on dirty (red-neck), tough questions. Not only in that chapter, but throughout his book, I felt Rubin used homosexuals and homosexuality incessantly and unhesitatingly as the scapegoats for his worst projections, which perpetuated most of the sensationalized clichés you're ever likely to hear on the matter. It's a marvel the distemper of that particular chapter didn't cause people to question his judgment in relation to the rest of the material. Rubin is hung-up on the simplistic idea that role-playing among gay lovers is merely an imitation of the roles Mommy and Daddy used to play in their marriage, in and out of bed. He doesn't seem to grasp that between any two males, there is a certain contest for supremacy and, if gay role-playing has any model, that's it. There is, of course, much more to it, which you will find out about in Chapter 3.

Nowhere, nowhere in Rubin's chapter "Male Homosexuality" does he ever touch upon the fact that between homosexual partners, there might be love.

Won't the so-called "homosexual revolution" change the fabric of American society as I know it?

Homosexuality is one of life's true mysteries. I believe its time has come. Such mysteries accomplish themselves—not without struggle certainly—but ultimately with grace: a frank acceptance of our busy, bartering, dying and breeding world. If you are agog for obvious change, you will be disappointed. In some least-expected moment, the reality and validity of homosexuality will slip through the barriers of prejudice and fear. It will suddenly appear at your side, a truly broader vision of human nature, of value to you for that, and in other ways this book will help you to discover.

Chapter 2

Gay Is

What is meant by this chapter heading?

I hope to show you in this chapter the external *physical* and inner *psychological* reality of homosexuality. Now that we have cleared the way for the evocation of your homosexual sensibility, let's take a look around. By "Gay Is" I mean that the phenomenon of homosexuality is observable around the country, and that being gay is in line with recent stated realizations about the nature of human nature.

What realizations?

Most significantly, the American Psychiatric Association's avowal that homosexuality is *not a mental disease*. This avowal was challenged, but the challenge failed and the avowed decision was confirmed by a referendum vote. The ramifications of this recognition of homosexuality as not a disease are far-reaching.

In what way?

In the implicit suggestion of the APA's decision that human nature, human *sexual* nature, is not twisted or evil if it expresses itself in its homosexual potential. In fact, human sexual nature is potentially straight *and* gay, as the great psychiatrists have been saying for years, albeit they sloughed over this minor detail in abstruse language, buried in the midst of long paragraphs. Even they, poor devils, had to accede to certain public codes if they wanted to see their work in print.

Does this mean that the old tourist, who drives by looking under the rim of the steering wheel, who is visor-capped, camera-bestraddled, and accompanied by his wife and five kids, might be gay?

Hard to believe, I know—but at the right time, in the right place, in the right atmosphere, and with the right partner, that harmless-looking old coot is potentially Oscar Wilde.

Further, this decision of the APA affords a new validity —social, legal, economic—to homosexuality; it is, at last, an unconcealed tip of the hat to one of the most enduring human phenomena, and one of the most persecuted of minorities.

I never *persecuted* homosexuals; how can you say that?

Perhaps you've never burned a "faggot" at the stake, but the manner in which you've been referring to gay people as "queers," etc., is subtle persecution. Even the most well intended literate and liberal individuals have thus unconsciously persecuted homosexuals, right along with the conscious persecution by Anita Bryant and other homophobics.

What are the ramifications of the APA's decision in regard to the straight world?

That decision indicates a change of attitude toward homosexuality by the straight world.

What is the change—what was the straight world's attitude toward homosexuals to begin with, and how did it evolve?

In the late 1940s and through the 1950s, the establishment considered gay as sick and extended tolerance. The Mattachine Society in particular (bless them) asked straight society to forbear in their treatment of homosexuals. After all, gay people, if they were sick—and mostly the Mattachine Society accepted that evaluation—should be treated as sick, and helped, not despised, and not set upon by rowdies. Magnanimously, straight people concurred.

What more could homosexuals ask?

Plenty. During the 1960s, and (need I remind you) the war in Vietnam, which drained off a good number of our young, including homosexuals who served, the idea began to take hold among caring people that perhaps homosexuals merited *acceptance*. The Kinsey Report with its irrefutable evidence of the large numbers of existing homosexuals, plus those who "indulged" now and then, had begun to sink in. Media news coverage with its swift and hungry need for material started to include gay activities (almost always for a laugh or a knock). And then gay people initiated meetings and with some degree of openness commiserated on their mutual difficulties. (It seemed a curious thing, even to them, to pledge alliance on the basis of their sexual adjustment, but it offered some "way" to proceed.)

Tolerance, yes; acceptance of homosexuality in general, perhaps, but not in my family, I'm sorry. Surely, that's as far as one can go with it, right?

Wrong—and I dislike using the word "wrong," but you are wrong on this occasion, and this is a book of straight answers and you would not get your money's worth if I were anything but frank with you.

You mean homosexuals want something beyond acceptance?

Yes, to be considered *equal*. In the words of Barbara Gittings, a gay lib true-leader, "What a homosexual wants, and here he is neither willing to compromise nor morally required to compromise—is acceptance of homosexuality as a way of life fully on a par with heterosexuality." This quote came from an essay by Miss Gittings. It was picked up in a 1975 fall issue of *Time* magazine, which devoted its cover to gay libber Air Force Sergeant Matlovitch, and its lead story to "The Gay Drive for Acceptance."

Social, legal, economic equality?

All three, and more.

More! But on what basis—what is there to justify such a claim?

Here we go back to the beginning of this chapter: Human nature is potentially straight and gay. Gay is one valid expression of that nature. Therefore in the course of that valid expression, homosexuals as American citizens are entitled to the recognition and guarantee of rights, as are all American citizens.

You mean people who are attracted erotically to members of their own sex are bucking to be entitled to the same rights as I have under the Bill of Rights?

Yes. By the way, your answer indicates that you still think of homosexuals in terms of their erotic attraction to members of their own sex, which is pragmatically correct. You're having difficulty conceiving them as human beings, just human beings, with the same range of emotions as your own.

But homosexuals love people of their own sex. I don't love people of my own sex to the extent of wanting to go to bed with them. How can it be said our emotional range is the same?

Again (page 18), I ask you—with the respect for your interest in this subject and your individuality—to think back and recall if there wasn't a moment, sometime, somewhere, when the possibility of falling in love with a member of your own sex consciously occurred to you. It may never have become overt; but that extreme feeling of closeness, of both peace and exaltation in the company of a member of your own sex so strong that you especially sought him/her out, is an experience almost everyone has had.

You're saying that that's homosexuality?

I'm saying that the potential existed, or exists in you. That homosexuals carry that same feeling to its final "term"—a feeling that but for a slight change of circumstance, *you* might have carried to its final "term." There is no qualitative difference in the feeling. Homosexuals simply follow through.

Suppose I can tell you honestly that I cannot ever remember entertaining such feelings. And since I can't, mustn't I refuse to consider homosexuals as equal, since in me there is no true point-of-identification?

I appreciate your honesty, as I hope you appreciate mine, and I realize that this is a tough subject. But if you cannot ever remember feeling as if you were falling in love with a member of your own sex, you are a rare person. I am not word-juggling or resorting to obscure authority when I tell you that if you tried, especially under the eye of a psychoanalyst, you could and would probably come up with a memory of such feelings. In short, in your heterosexual existence, such feelings are, to say the least, inappropriate, and you have repressed them.

Then to all practical purposes these feelings do not exist in me and I am correct in refusing homosexuals a point-of-identification in my own psyche, therefore equality, am I not?

You have articulated precisely the point of view that stands in direct opposition to my own, and to most homosexuals, and to those heterosexuals who would grant homosexuals equality. I salute you for it.

And you can't answer it?

I feel the answer is beyond the scope of this book.

But if I admit to you that way back in public school I recall a close friendship and mutual-masturbatory experience with a boy I used to pal around with?

Then I would say that at least once, and in small part, you did experience homosexual feelings, and you are now in a position to agree to a psychic *point-of-identification* with gay people. For which, again, I salute you. That "identification" is the "more" that gay people want now.

But I believed such feelings were wrong; weren't they?

Perhaps such feelings were wrong for you (and if you are speaking of any time more than ten years ago, society would have concurred that such feelings were wrong, sick, sinful). And perhaps such feelings are wrong *for you today*, and if you did experience a homosexual urge right now, you would clamp down on it.

But society is changing its attitude toward homosexuality, as I have indicated; and that is based largely on the *evolving conception of human nature as bisexual*. The authorities, revered in their judgment of the right and wrong of gay sex, are broken idols: smashed in part by the Kinsey Report. But the rightness or the wrongness of it is a matter of personal standard: not under discussion. If you think still that it is wrong to permit yourself such feelings, even for a minute, that is your prerogative. But you must admit to the emotional "family of man" homosexuals whose emotional/sexual promptings you *have* felt, and you must admit their right to act upon those feelings if that is their standard for themselves, and if it does not interfere with your standard for yourself. In short, gay people are people with human feelings, not weird beings from outer space.

So if, for the sake of argument, I admit the minutest experience of having felt homosexual emotion, I have made a point-of-identification with gay people?

You have.

Well, if that's all there is to it, why the fuss?

Because people are afraid that if they go even that far, they will be accused of homosexuality: worst of all they will accuse themselves of it.

Okay. I can conceive homosexual emotion at the furthest end of my emotional range. But is there more required of me to assimilate the homosexual sensibility?

Only a projection, in imagination, of the experience of what it is to be a homosexual living in America today: particularly the joy of it, the sense of fulfillment and freedom and integrity homosexuals have begun to feel. In short the liberated homosexual's way of looking at things.

But I don't know that. What is it like to be gay? How can I conceive the homosexual's way of looking at things?

Through *this* book. *Incidentally, your question is the first real and important question any inquirer into the subject must ask: What is it like to be gay?* Just asking the question—and not coming on with a chip on your shoulder—is a true start toward understanding.

Have other heterosexuals taken this step toward understanding homosexuality? Toward granting equality to homosexuals?

Few grant the equality, but it is not far off if events proceed as they have. Heterosexuals are making an effort to understand—abetted by the determination of gay lib people to be understood, accepted, and treated as equals. Let's look more closely at that *Time* magazine lead article, labeled on the magazine cover: "The Gay Drive for Acceptance," across a head-and-shoulders photo of Sergeant Matlovitch.

Who is Sergeant Matlovitch?

An Air Force man who won the highest medals for bravery, and was seriously wounded during the Vietnam war.

Why did he make the *Time* cover?

For suing the Air Force over his discharge from service because of his open declaration of homosexuality.

You mean he wanted to get back in service, even as a declared homosexual?

Yes, why not; he wanted to prove that a homosexual—and many fought in the war—could be as loyal and effective a military man as any heterosexual. It came as something of a surprise to the middle- and upper-middle-class readers of the magazine. The fact that *Time* featured Sergeant Matlovitch, and commissioned the lead article to be written, is, in itself, evidence that men of goodwill want to understand the homosexual "greening of America."

What is meant by the homosexual "greening of America"?

Ah, I was hoping you'd ask that! We have in this chapter covered some of the inner difficulty heterosexuals have in trying to understand homosexuals, and we'll come back to that subject until it is thrashed out. But, as per your question, let's examine what's happening in the land in an exterior sense as regards homosexuality.

First, *The Greening of America* was a book in the sixties that described the peculiar, creative, spontaneous emergence of young people all over the country—as flower children, interested in peace and love and mystic contemplation. These sensitive young people simply appeared on the scene everywhere suddenly; no movement grew, there was seemingly no gradual spread of ideas; their philosophy emerged virtually full-blown, a springlike greening of spirituality. Their philosophy resisted everything that Vietnam stood for: violence, imperialism, the death or maiming of themselves and their friends. Everywhere young people, and many mature ones, felt the same emotions in concert, and in concert expressed themselves.

When I say the homosexual "greening of America," I mean to indicate that gay awareness—consciousness raising, if you prefer—is emerging all over the country in a similar fashion. Not quite so spontaneously as the first "greening," but everywhere and strongly people are coming to realize that gay *is*, that a relative, friend, or business associate is gay—and that you simply cannot any longer hide your head as to the reality of it nor remain superstitious concerning it. That homosexuality must be taken into consideration as a valid life-style for some, if not for oneself.

Let me say that the seeds of this idea were planted years ago. "Students of the homosexual movement" trace its beginnings back to the 1940s, and even earlier. There were some gay organizations in existence even during Senator Joe McCarthy's purge in the fifties. These were underground pioneer groups of great courage, which did not, however, liberate most of us.

You said that the homosexual "greening of America" was not quite so spontaneous as the first "greening." How did the present homosexual "greening" begin?

With a police raid on a gay dance bar in New York's West Village called the Stonewall, on the balmy summer evening of June 28, 1969.

Don't such raids occur often?

Yes, but this one was different.

How?

The police swaggered in as usual, shoved the customers around, shouted for the manager, jeered the go-go boys in cages behind the bar, and roughed up the bartenders. They ordered the customers out, but this time something happened. The gay patrons did leave the bar, but they gathered across the street. The rage that had been accumulating in them for decades, especially the decade of Vietnam, finally found its voice. They shouted back at the cops, trading obscenity for obscenity, giving as good as they got; they pelted the police with coins. They blocked the street with their riot of indignation. The police took refuge inside the bar from the two hundred or more angry gay people who, instead of slinking away from such a scene, as they customarily do, had, this night, banded together and fought back. Police vans arrived, scores were arrested—gays and police bruised and cut. The newspapers picked up the story, and for a change the publicity coverage included the gay side of the incident. To this day, gay participants at Stonewall display their scars with pride. If you happened to have been there, you're almost a gay saint.

And the upshot?

The riot at Stonewall became an overt symbol of gay liberation. It united a growing feeling among gay people that the unjustness with which they had always been treated needed redress. In obvious ways their American civil rights were being wantonly violated and they hadn't done a damned thing about it. The incident, and the curious, spontaneous national bias in their favor, began what has amounted to a gay civil revolt. The kids that night at Stonewall spoke and acted for millions of homosexuals around the country.

Surely, that single incident did not cause people to come pouring "out of the closet"?

Once again, I see you know the vernacular, which again reassures me that another gay glossary is not required. To answer your question, no, people did not come pouring out of the closets as they have in the years since. As a gay college professor friend of mine confided, "I read about it, and I wouldn't want to have been there because if my name had been published, I'd have lost my tenure. But believe me, a door in my heart opened, and a feeling of warmth toward those Stonewall kids filled it." I don't quite know why this reaction among gay and straight people alike was widespread. It was: and gay people have kept the faith by a nationwide yearly celebration of gay lib day on June 28—1977 marked the eighth anniversary. There are parades in the big cities. The parade in New York gathers on Christopher Street—on the very street in the Village, in front of the very bar (now unoccupied) where it all began. They march several thousand together in a mood of great good humor up Sixth Avenue between crowds (for the most part friendly and amused) along the sidewalks to a mall in Central Park, where the crowd is addressed by gay leaders. It is truly a celebration. I have been to these celebrations on the mall; almost ten thousand gay people, many with their arms around each other—their pride in themselves as human beings who happen to be gay evident. It is beautiful, and I use that word as carefully as I use the word "love." (I believe that beauty is simply reality seen with the eyes of love.) I looked out over those legions of people, young mostly (but many not so young), and I reminded myself that they were here not to demand contracts or votes or money—they were here in the cause of love. It would have been a hard heart that wasn't moved to tears.

Aside from the warmth felt by your professor friend, and your tears, what did Stonewall accomplish?

It gave brave gay people impetus to organize. The Gay Activist Alliance got started with meetings and dances in a refurbished New York City fire house, which alas, burned mysteriously in 1974. But it regrouped. There were many other organizations birthed by Stonewall, most notably, The National Gay Task Force, which I will tell you about in Chapter 15. Brave gay groups began meeting on campuses.

In what way were the organized gay people brave?

Who could predict red-neck reaction to a bunch of freaks getting together to assert their civil rights? Brave gays resisted their apprehension about being set upon in the street or invaded in a meeting hall by rowdies. Also, gays braced themselves against unprovoked police brutality, anyplace, anytime. Fiery fracases ensued. But as the old alchemists said: No transmutation without fire—no cross, no crown.

Why do you call them freaks? How did the police respond ultimately?

Although the kids in the Stonewall riot were not poorly dressed, gay people thereafter who proceeded to carry the ball for Gay Lib tended to dress down: beards, dungarees, boots. The new prophets were strictly informal, if not disheveled. My appellation "freaks" is an affectionate one. The straight world considered them freaks as much for what they were about as for what they looked like: united on the basis of their homosexual proclivities—madness! Ambush them! Beat them into submission! Shortly after Stonewall, American police-state tactics flared and never have gay people more resembled early Christians in the sense of literally being hounded and persecuted at gatherings. But the American check-and-balance of power also worked: once the legal precedent for assemblage was established, meetings of gay people proceeded peacefully, at least as far as the police were concerned. Freaks no more!

Did gay organizations on campus fare any better?

Yes—less violence, but still those college authorities to contend with. Sanction for gay people to meet was finally granted but with utmost reluctance. I like to picture the facial expressions of the presidents of Rutgers, Columbia, Harvard, Yale, and even Princeton when they *had* to agree, not only to let gay clubs form on campus, but that legally the gay organizations had the right to hold *dances!* Dances? Dances!—in which boys dance with boys, disco music blares, the lights flash, and males kiss males, usually when the dancing is through. The old grads, when informed of it or actually seeing it, must have dropped their teeth. For those of us who spent years of suffering in silence and self-hatred in college, it is a welcome sight.

My own university, Colgate, wrote to me—in reply to my letter to them about forming a gay club—that at Colgate there may be some homosexuals among the faculty and in the student body, but as yet no one had come forward to request the formation of any such organization, so they saw no need for one. I'll pay a visit to that old campus one of these days . . . look out!

Were there other manifestations of this homosexual "greening of America" as you call it?

I must not give you the impression that Stonewall was an isolated instance; in its wake, there was a week of severe unrest among gay people in New York and around the country. But mostly gay people staged hastily organized, peaceful demonstrations and sang, "We Shall Overcome." Nor must I give the impression that the gay organizations I mentioned, and the campus gay organizations, were the only ones that sprang up. Gays in every city of any size "got themselves together," and by gays, I mean gay boys *and* gay girls, and each group picked a name they intended as an emblem of defiance of the establishment, such as the Cocksucker Tribe or Planned Nonparenthood or the Lavender Menace. Gays sported T-shirts with "Butch" or "Femme" emblazoned across the front. As I've said, gay people had a new look generally—*not* the limp-wristed, wan-voiced, too-tightly-dressed "queer" look; but a virile, dungaree and T-shirt and booted look with plenty of muscle showing literally and figuratively.

Organizations that were spur-of-the-moment affairs began to meet regularly and follow formal agendas. One of the best of these, and one with which I am personally acquainted, is the Gay Academic Union: teachers from all levels of schooling—with the courage to appear publicly at their own meetings or at meetings of other gay organizations (and the courage to resist "reports" of their having attended such meetings). At the Academic Union sessions, a gay topic of discussion is planned, and it is thrashed out thoroughly; I can see where a kind of new morality for homosexuals is beginning to form that will take into consideration the needs of the new homosexual in this new era.

As for gay publications, it would seem anybody with ten cents turned to print, and as a result hundreds of gay lib papers and magazines flourished for a few issues and went bankrupt—many were called but in this case, again, few were chosen. But the publications that have survived are prodigious: The *Los Angeles Advocate, Mandate,* gay community newspapers, and some dozen others. They are professionally art-directed and edited, and offer national coverage of the gay scene. The combined influence of several of these periodicals in the area of criticism can—like *The New York Times*—help or hurt a book, play, picture, etc., on a gay theme; also, to some degree influence the election or defeat of a political candidate who comes out one way or the other for gay rights.

Still another manifestation of the homosexual "greening of America"—the gay people who established work communes, coffeehouses, community centers (often called drop-in centers), and "love-ins" (just gay get-togethers for the hell of it).

Of serious long-term concern to the new homosexuals: the organization and pressure of a number of homosexuals in any particular state to lobby in the state legislature for the repeal of old sodomy laws, to be replaced by new laws inaugurating nondiscriminatory guidelines for homosexuals in the areas of sex, jobs, housing, and even government positions. This activity has been implemented recently by David Goodstein, *Los Angeles Advocate* editor, who is presently putting together a group to lobby Congress in Washington for similar *national* legislation.

As an aftermath of Stonewall, a strong religious movement grew among gay people. There is now a gay church, open to all of course, but started by and for gay people, called the Metropolitan Community Church, and a parish can be found in almost every large city. This church was founded by a man named Troy Perry and he wrote a book about it called *The Lord Is My Shepherd and He Knows I'm Gay*. And then I must mention that in book publishing, legitimate houses are now doing books at a profit for a specifically gay audience, and books at a profit for a general audience in the fields of fiction or nonfiction about gay people.

The theater has not been idle. Purely gay plays and revues have deposited their jot of merriment and departed. One I liked, and that spoke of the truths, realities, and unrealities of the emotional lives of homosexuals—as is my primary plan in *Straight Answers*—was called *Lovers*. It dared to portray "role-playing" in a seriocomic skit. The *emotional truths* of gay role-playing are complicated and partly for that reason are rarely presented in any form. *Lovers* did it fine.

So, there have been many manifestations of that homosexual "greening of America"—and probably more are yet to surface. Gay life is a subculture, of course, but it has already made a significant contribution of freedom from guilt for millions, which is certainly enough to justify it.

I have only one serious regret, and I believe that regret is shared by a number of gay people.

You regret what?

That the straight world, everybody in it, was made to seem the enemy, was polarized against gay people. The real enemy? Always superstition, and prejudiced thinking and feeling. The gay world did itself a disfavor if, indeed, it seemed to proclaim a blanket accusation against straight people. But I suppose that during even a civil revolt (strikes, for instance) few of the participants are concerned about public relations. Perhaps this book will mend some fences.

How?

By showing that you, as a straight person, had much to gain, have much to gain by gay liberation.

Such as?

A portion of the citizenry released from fear, released for a true expression of its individuality, without which, I'm told, a democratic society cannot function. And then there is the matter of the personal benefit to you of a direct description of the homosexual sensibility.

What is meant by "direct"?

Homosexuals in many fields have affected your life for years, but rarely, if ever, have they spoken out in person and told you that their ability/skill/aptitude/talent in their field—which they put at your disposal—was founded on a way of looking at life divergent from your own; on a range of feelings that exist in everyone but are not acknowledged often by heterosexuals; on a set of premises about human nature which exactly complement your own, but of which you have preferred to remain unaware. You may have been somewhat aware of the fact that a product or service or work of talent or an aptitude in some special field, of value to you, sprang from a source you could not imagine, nor identify. But that has been as close as you were able to get to the homosexual sensibility. It is as close as homosexuals dared let you get, lest you be offended. But more on this later. We are covering in this chapter the subject of what it is like to be gay now, in America, since the homosexual "greening" of the country began.

Aren't you being pretty damned oblique yourself about this sensibility?

You're right, I am. But the only way I can conceive of to tell you about it *straight* is by conundrum, paradox, and antithesis. Oblique methods, indeed, but has ever the truth about a thing been approximated in any better manner? The picture of the homosexual sensibility will form for you slowly, as we go, and you will feel it, and you will enjoy it, and it will enhance your life. But we are only at the beginning of our consideration of what it is like to be gay, a necessary prelude to your comprehension. The framework of this chapter concerns the recent homosexual greening of America, the fact that *Gay is*.

All right. How has this phenomenon affected your own life-style?

It has released me enough to write a book for gay people called *Gay Spirit*, in the course of which I was able to describe some of the things about gay life that were amusing, and to speak of some aspects of gay life that offered problems. The book resulted in fear-lessening for gay people and a catharsis for myself. An established publisher would not easily have taken on such a book before gay lib. I made some money out of what had been my darkest secret. I was able to put my homosexual sensibility to work directly.

Personally, my life has been farmed clear of those gay friends who are hypocritical about their own homosexuality, or about mine. I regret losing them, of course. But they are of an older gay world, and they still believe that if they make a supreme effort to hide their homosexuality, they can live in their social and financial environment more safely. Perhaps they're right, about themselves.

As to myself, I have never made any great effort to hide my homosexuality. I suppose there was a conviction in me that my straight friends were privately amused by my being gay; it was the intangible part of my personality that intrigued. On the other hand, I never made an effort to let people know that I was gay, and that got me in trouble now and again. Something else: I never thought that homosexuality was the primary point of relationship with anyone except a lover. It always seemed to me that I had plenty to talk about with friends, straight or gay, and that it was this larger part of life that we had in common. I think, among my straight friends, I lost mostly those who were in the process of raising small children. I guess they believe that gay is catchy. Maybe when the children are grown, we'll get back together. Maybe.

How did you manage to write two novels in which there is little homosexual reference?

I transposed gay males into females and vice-versa, streets into avenues, apartments into houses, and several times I assembled a character out of the living characteristics of three or four different people, of both sexes.

Would you claim that that character transposition of gender is honest?

Art, even fiction-writing if you're serious about it as I am, is not life: It is verisimilitude. The Real, in both art and life, is what works. I start writing a piece of fiction with the idea in mind of an emotional effect that I hope to evoke in the general reader—exactly as I am writing this book, as a matter of fact, with the hope of evoking in you a feeling for your own homosexual sensibility. In this book, which is nonfiction, however, it is against the rules to arrange matters for dramatic purposes. I feel that in fiction the *only* rule is to arrange matter for dramatic purposes, and I have done it. You see, *I* know, as I believe most people do not, that a homosexual experiences the same emotions as a heterosexual—granted, the object of one's love is a male, not a female, but *the emotions are the same*. Therefore, in the writing of fiction, transposition of character is necessary so that the *side issue* of homosexuality is not raised; matters are arranged in order that the heterosexual or general reader may feel what the writer designed his story for the reader to feel. A piece of fiction must be judged on how well the writer succeeded in that, and whether or not the articulated emotion was worth the trouble in the first place.

Now that *Gay is*, will the transposition of character continue?

Yes. It will take years for readers to realize that gay emotion is the same as straight emotion. Gay writers for straight audiences will keep on transposing their characters, ducking the side issue. But there have been serious writers, gay and straight, of books and movies, too, who've risked a limited audience, and accepted the consequent limited financial return, to write about specifically homosexual experience. They are up against tough barriers. In the case of movies the first barrier is to get produced. Producers who share an unconcern over limited returns are not easy to find. Second, with an exception or two (such as the movie *Sunday, Bloody Sunday*), somehow writers of gay material aren't often able to extract from it (what is the phrase?) enduring human values. They themselves are too often sidetracked by the outward specialness of gay material and unable to elevate it, raise it from the particular to general human experience, so that everyone in the audience, not only the gay segment, can feel the emotions involved. That is a perennial problem of artists in any field; for the writer of gay material, the problem is compounded.

What do you think of gay material presently circulating?

Too little of it; despite what might seem to the outsider as a deluge of literary and theatrical concern with homosexuality, little of quality is being produced. And then the books about it, oh dear. . . .

Medical doctors and doctors of the psyche write books based largely on the histories of people they've treated. They draw a pathetic picture of the homosexual in society. Or if they avoid that obstacle, they are poor writers. However effective they may be as healers, they deal in anything but plain English; they have pet theories couched in the language of doctoral dissertations and whatever it is constructive they have to say is lost on a general reader.

Clergymen and educators sometimes risk a volume, and it is usually a plea for tolerance aimed at the parents of gay children. But the idea that homosexuals are sick—if not evil—somehow sneaks through in their writing, and they have unwittingly perpetuated the transformation of homosexuality from heresy into illness. Nicer, but still demeaning to gay people. The general reader yawns.

There are the militant books by recently declared gay people or gay people active in the gay lib movement. Their intention is always laudable: Gay is good, gay is proud, and maintain your gay spirit are all good thoughts. But the writing is so young: acres and acres of prose unrelieved by a trace of humor, unburdened by subtlety, ardently overstated, accusatory in tone of straight people, if not fanatically proselytizing. This kind of writing (or speaking) has led crusading *Los Angeles Advocate* editor David Goodstein to comment on the split between the silent majority of gay people and these far-out presumed gay spokespeople. The latter, Goodstein has said, are "disconnected from their constituency" by the fact of such jejune writing. The general reader is appalled.

In the last category of writing on homosexuality, the writer, gay or straight, tries to *edify* the general reader. Is there much about homosexuality of a purely factual nature that hasn't been thoroughly explored? It seems to me the general reader has been edified and bored to death with the knowledge of the meaning of a red handkerchief hanging out of the left rear dungaree pants pocket; that he has been edified, and sorrowed along with the mother who found out about her son's homosexuality in *Consenting Adults*; has been edified by Merle Miller, who outlines his difficulties with declared homosexuality in *On Being Different* (in which he tells about "finding out" about himself, and everybody else "finding out" about him). Cleanly written. You know what he felt. Edifying.

My ongoing caveat with homosexual material expressly intended for the general heterosexual reader is that never have I come across a book that offers you, personally, beyond edification, a specific *benefit*: a genuine *something* that could add to your well-being today! The writing I have read does not put at your immediate disposal the one thing about homosexuality that you might really use: the creative potential in you of *your homosexual sensibility*.

What goes on in a gay bar?

Cruising, for sure. There are many kinds of gay bars. The patrons of all of them, however, are on the lookout for someone who arouses their concupiscence—or someone in whom they themselves arouse concupiscence. But a lot else goes on: cheery visiting with friends; exchanging a few words (of curiosity) with strangers; dancing. But mostly, standing around with a glass in hand, grooving on the whole scene.

What are the different kinds of gay bars?

Gay bars totaled a handful in any one city until the late sixties when the fact of homosexuality broke free, and then, in typically American fashion, tastes became specialized and special bars opened to cater to those tastes. In each case, the designation of the bar describes the chief, though by no means exclusive, taste of most of its patrons. There are: leather bars, dance bars, juice bars (orange, etc.), neighborhood dives aplenty, hustler bars, wrinkle-rooms (elderly gays congregate), bars for blacks and ethnics, transvestite bars as opposed to drag and drag-show bars, servicemen bars, hippie bars, collegiate bars, elegant bars, country-queen bars (in the country, among my favorites), quiet bars and noisy bars (distinguishable chiefly for those characteristics), sing-a-long bars, cocktail-hour bars (as opposed to bars busy strictly in the wee hours), show-time bars, mixed bars (gay and straight), lesbian bars, rough-trade bars (as opposed to highly organized and congenial-hustler bars), junky bars where serious addicts go, motorcycle bars (where a six-to-ten-thousand-dollar bike is your major entree ticket), theater-people bars and ballet-dancer bars (much overlapping here), resort place bars, piano bars (patrons sit around the piano while one entertainer plays), hideaway bars (way off on a back street in the shrubbery; only a jammed parking lot betrays its nature), orgy bars (in the back room), supper-club bars, private bars (with yearly dues). Then there are huge bars which contain several different kinds of bars in one building, and bars so small as to accommodate only a couple of dozen people.

Does the Mafia run these bars?

I think in the larger cities, some of the larger bars may be Mafia-owned. The Mafia as an owner of gay bars has two things to be said about it. One: Up until recently, the Mafia sense of interior decor has been nil. Any old shack would serve, and though it might be jammed with gay people spending freely, the Mafia did not, as it were, plow back much money into improving the plant. Second: if the Mafia runs a bar, that bar is usually the safest place in town for gay people. I have never heard of *any* incident between a Mafia person and a gay person. Mafia places are models of smooth, if impersonal management. A raid on a Mafia bar is rare, and a raid without warning beforehand is almost nonexistent. The Mafia takes care of its own, and the bitterest attacks on Mafia-run operations have never mentioned the Mafia's (I should think profitable) handling of gay bars.

What happens at a gay beach?

Bar life transposed to the seashore. A great deal of just looking at good physiques with comments; a lot of walking by the waterside; not a great deal of drinking; a lot of picnicking (the same sun which broils straight people often broils gay people); appreciation of beach wear and equipment if it's elaborate or stylish; an occasional drag queen with a hat or a sari, to everyone's amusement; rather a lot of getting-to-know the gay people on the nearest beach blanket; much concern over towering clouds on the horizon; sudden congealing into companionship of large groups and departure from the beach in a caravan of cars to someone's house for continuation of the party mood and then serious pairing off for sex or an amicable and spontaneous orgy (the best kind).

If I were gay, what would happen to me at a gay bath?

You must understand that at a gay bath, the *un*conscious rules your behavior (to be uptight at a bath is to destroy the experience for yourself and others). A word or gesture may be exchanged, but otherwise it is mostly unspoken experience. You must also know that baths are dark places, wet places, serious-sex places. A cardinal rule of etiquette is: *No giggling*. Giggling might be interpreted by a heavy old gentleman passing by as a put-down of him. Every one of us is vulnerable about an imperfection somewhere on our anatomy—and at the baths, putting-down is not done. A refusal of attention is usually couched in a soft "no thanks" or a gentle breaking of someone's grip on your genitals.

You stretch out on the bed in the cubicle you've rented, and leave the door open. Passersby on little cat feet (or so it sounds: a great deal of pitter-pat of bare feet in baths) will peer in at you. If he likes what he sees, or you like him, he edges farther in through the door and you undrape the towel around your waist (which everybody wears) continuing to gesture him in. If neither likes what he sees, of course, there is a fast turnabout on his part and you look bored or close your eyes in dismissal. If he likes what he sees, and you don't, you must make clear to him that you've just had it, sorry, and that you left the door open by mistake. If you like what you see but he doesn't and leaves, ah, that is the moment at the "tubs" when life can be difficult. You either chase after him (he has disappeared down corridors more shaded and labyrinthian than even Emily Dickinson was used to), or you wait patiently for the next peerer-into-your-cubicle who appeals to you (and after a turndown one's demands lessen) or you masturbate: poor in a place where everyone else seems rich. Or you hie yourself to the orgy room where it is so dark you are simply, wildly lost in a tangle of arms, legs, mouths, etc., on wall-to-wall foam rubber.

Gay baths have caught on: The venerable Continental Baths in New York has a barbershop, a food shop, and several other kinds of shops—and a stage where some fairly decent entertainers perform: Bette Midler made her debut there. (Gay Talese did research there for his long-awaited book on sex.) The show-time audience just sits or stands around wearing those waist towels (always skimpy) and they pay strict attention to the stage for the hour the show is on. When the show is over, they repair to the highly chlorinated pool, or the steam room, or the showers which are placed with originality helter-skelter along the corridors, or back to their cubicles.

You can live at the Continental for weeks on end if you can afford it, and never go out. It's amazing, too, how the very young have made it a home. I am told of high-school boys who bunk there quasi-permanently and who receive morning calls when it is time to get up and get ready for school, and are provided with a sandwich for lunch from one of the arcade shops!

Are there other businesses run for and by gay people?

Judging from the ads in gay newspapers and magazines, I would say by now that a homosexual in a large city could tend to all his needs and wants as a civilized person from businesses run by and for gay people. Besides the gay boutiques and gay restaurants and gay hotels, he can even book himself on an exclusive all-gay Caribbean cruise ship. *The New York Times* Travel section took note of such a trip a while back. Everyone seemed to enjoy it.

What about straight people who patronize such businesses or who drink at a gay bar, aren't they just slumming?

I suppose some are. Let's consider my friends Joe and Vivian. Along with their twelve-year-old son and intermittent visits from two older children, Joe and Vivian ensconce themselves in Provincetown, Massachusetts, at an all-gay motel called The Boatslip. Vivian and her young son stay the entire summer, while Joe, a real estate broker, travels up from their place in New York City and stays a long weekend. Joe is a good-natured man in his late forties, rides a bicycle on these weekends to reduce his paunch, and is interested in Oriental philosophy. Vivian, a tall, slim woman with her blonde hair pulled tightly in a bun, dresses stunningly. They are the sort of people you would more probably meet in the Hamptons. Yet Vivian, especially, sits each bright shiny day on the Boatslip deck (sunbathers and Pina Colada drinkers) blending harmoniously with the gay life around her, and her twelve-year-old romps in the pool having a grand time. At cocktail hour, she removes to the glassed-in deck bar where the disco-dancing surges.

Joe and Vivian have together and separately a crowd of gay friends, and when Joe is in New York, Vivian has a host of gay admirers to escort her to dinner at the Boatslip or around town for entertainment and dinner elsewhere. Indeed, you will find such couples in increasing numbers at gay resorts everywhere. They are not slumming. I made a point of asking Vivian just what they did get out of their summers at the Boatslip.

"My God," she said, "we used to go to straight resorts and we were bored to death. If anyone spoke to us, it was the worst casual clichés about where we were, what we ate, the weather, and so forth. Here, everybody speaks to us, everybody is so handsome, our son adores the place as do the other children. Both Joe and I feel when we're sitting on that deck with all those gay people just waves of love washing over us. And *we* feel loved, and important, have real conversations about life, and when we get back to New York in the fall, we feel we've really been somewhere. The closest summer experience to it that we've known was one time we spent on the French Riviera. I guess people have to be sophisticated in order to risk showing and sharing emotion—we find that in our summers here."

I don't think Vivian's statement indicated that she and Joe were slumming. I do think that they have accepted the fact that *Gay is*, and that they are deriving personal pleasure from their fully developed homosexual sensibilities.

Chapter 3

Role-Playing

Isn't homosexual role-playing just like Dr. Rubin said: gay people imitating heterosexual husbands and wives?

Only in that two individuals are involved in a love and sex relationship. Gay role-playing is different, it is distinct, and it is founded on no imitation. If you are to enjoy the benefits of your homosexual sensibility, it is vital that you understand what it is like to be gay. That has been our quest, begun in the previous chapter. Now, as we begin the chapter on homosexual role-playing, which is in my estimation *not the only but the single most important key* to the comprehension of gay sex and love phenomena, I would ask you to put aside Dr. Rubin's misleading theories. Clear your mind, in fact, of all that you may project of heterosexual love and sex, and consider with me gay love and sex as *an* "other" experience.

I thought you said that homosexuality was an extension of the normal range of human feeling, that heterosexuals also had the potential of gay emotions?

I did say that, and I meant it. Homosexual feelings are potential in everyone. But when homosexual emotions are not only

51

felt but *expressed*, one enters a new dimension of human experience in which new distinctions must be made.

What distinctions?

Such as the object of homosexual love and sex is a male, and that fact means that the exercise of eroticism is going to take place almost entirely in a dimension populated by males.

How does male/female role-playing operate between two males?

I'll answer that in a minute. You do still insist, I notice, on the male/female comparison. I stress that it doesn't hold; it is role-playing *between two males*, clearly equipped as males and living as males in the world. But let me provide you with terms gay people use. There are a number (in ascending grades of intensity): giver-receiver, top man-bottom man, dominant-submissive, butch-femme, master-slave, sadist-masochist, and no doubt others. I prefer the terms "dominant-submissive," as seeming to describe gay relationships *at the midpoint of intensity*. I conclude this from my own experience, and from the frequent use of these terms in the personal column ads of gay publications. "S" and "M" are also used frequently, as a description of restricted relationships, however. (A desire for a mutual or equal relationship is delineated in a statement by the advertiser that he seeks, or is willing to give, a relationship of "sincere sharing.")

This subject of role-playing and the terms used to refer to it is a touchy one, even among gay people. For me, "dominant" and "submissive" are apt designations of the two major gay role-playing stances. But the words are often misinterpreted by both gay people and straight people. No judgment is intended by these terms. The problem is equating "dominant" with masculinity, which is considered desirable, and "submissive" with femininity, which has been traditionally considered undesirable and a put-down.

Refuting such preconceptions and absurd prejudices is what women's lib and gay lib are all about.

Isn't this getting complicated?

Yes. If you want to make a dent in the subject of gay role-playing, you've got to be prepared for *complication*. One reason few straight people understand it—and many gay people don't—is that they're unwilling to be patient with its complicatedness. I call role-playing *the gay theory of relativity* for that reason. Still, if you will bear with me as I make the necessary distinctions in terms and in sexual activities, I believe a "pattern in the carpet" will begin to emerge, and you will better comprehend the subject in its many aspects.

There is another important distinction: When I say that a homosexual is "dominant," I always prefix it with the term "more-than-not"; ditto for the "submissive" homosexual. That little phrase covers a lot of territory. It means submissive or dominant most of the time with most sexual partners, but not all the time with every partner. In gay life, there is a good deal of switching of roles, depending on the time, place, partner at hand and the "atmosphere" in which a connection is made. I will explain "atmosphere" later. It has been my effort to bring to gay people consciousness of their own role-playing in the belief that honesty with themselves about it will save them from misguided alliances, infidelity, consequent emotional upheaval, and then the long lonely love-searches, isolation, disillusion, bitterness.

Does a homosexual consider himself "dominant" or "submissive"?

You are ready then to begin to grapple with the specifics of role-playing. The answer to your question is: If he's wise, he has knowledge of his more-than-not erotic needs, and when he goes out cruising, he will eliminate automatically those individuals who will not fulfill those needs.

How does he arrive at any conception of his needs?

That question requires a rough outline of what I have observed of the three stages of homosexual erotic development.

I emphasize rough, because what happens is rarely clear-cut: (1) mishmash, (2) mirror images, (3) opposites.

1. Sex among the young is a *mishmash*. Anybody jumps in bed with anybody they like and *each partner does what pleases himself*. They fellate one another, they penetrate one another anally (which are the two major gay sexual stances), and they do a number of other things with one another *in a great spirit of freedom*. At the end, both lie back exhausted, until their young glands are rested, and then they go at it again, "for days," as the kids say. Certainly, in mishmash sex of the young, there is no distinguishable role-playing. Which, alas, leads the young to despise and reject what they call role-playing labels. They believe from *their* experience that that is what sex is like and will always be like, and that it is wrong to separate out any feature of it and slap on a label. If that was what sex is always like, a mishmash, they'd be right. *But, as one grows older, other sexual considerations press forward*. It doesn't bother the kids, by the way, that mishmash sex (when a relationship is founded upon it and the lovers cohabit) seems quickly to evaporate in terms of interest of one or both partners, and of course, someone is abandoned. Loss of early love is "The Pits," but not for long.

2. The second stage, as I see it, and an obvious outgrowth of the first, happens when homosexual partners want and find *mirror images* of one another. Out cruising at this stage, they seek, consciously or not, someone who shares their own interests—and partners, indeed, who are physically look-alikes with themselves. This time their sex is *determinedly mutual*. If mutuality is not achieved, and one or the other is left unsatisfied (again, I assume cohabitation by them on the basis of their love), cracks begin to appear in the relationship.

I would place this stage in time when both lovers are in their mid- to late twenties, certainly after they've both had a half dozen years of mishmash. The cracks translate themselves into strangely motivated arguments, even violence. What they are doing, unbeknownst to themselves, is pitting ego against ego for more-than-not dominance—or they wake up one morning totally sexually disinterested in one another, realizing that they are "sisters" really, or *both* more-than-not submissive.

Either way, again new sexual considerations have pressed forward from the unconscious and ruined their sex together, which converts into a ruined living arrangement. Occasionally they become good friends, and for the sake of their mutually convenient living quarters, continue—but only as roommates. Mostly, they break up.

3. I postulate a third stage for gay people (again these stages may overlap, regress, remain static or be skipped—I am constructing a model so that we may grasp unseen components, as a model of the atom was constructed so as to grasp its unseen components). I should say that around the age of thirty one looks back over his sexual experience and discovers that one's primary satisfaction has been achieved by playing with a partner either the more-than-not dominant or the more-than-not submissive role. Then, out cruising, one seeks one's *opposite* in terms of those needs of one's own which are primary. A submissive gay seeks a dominant one, etc.

That kind of complementary relationship is based on psychological soil which has the substance to nourish and maintain two lovers, in my experience. Homosexual love relationships—always difficult for reasons objective to either partner, as well as subjective problems each may have—*established on the basis of complementary sexual and emotional requirements have a chance of enduring*.

There are those gay people who abominate the idea of one partner with whom to share the deepest and the most of life, who enjoy their promiscuity and wouldn't sacrifice it for anything. Perhaps. But I think the search for one partner is an elementary need in the foundation layers of the human psyche, and true for most of us.

It may be that those individual gay people who inveigh against description of themselves as either more-than-not dominant or more-than-not submissive are about equally balanced in their sexual preference, or immersed in work that allows little flow of libidinous energy into sexual channels in any event.

Of course, some gay people are *incapable of self-examination* and inference from their own experience—and go on, as such people are doomed to do, making the same mistakes over and over. They chase a chimeric love-ideal down the nights and days with no luck since that ideal is usually unsuited to their real sexual needs. Hence, one motivation of compulsive cruising for which gay life is so famous. Sadly, for those unaware people, gay life is composed of a thousand beginnings.

A gay person, by observing his emotional/erotic experience

through these (3) approximate stages, arrives at a rough idea of his major sexual role-orientation.

Suppose two gay people with complementary sexual needs do get together and live together—does each play his role exclusively, in and out of bed?

It is my belief that role-playing should be limited to the *bedroom where it works*. Out of bed, it can be done, if agreed upon by both lovers. But out of bed I'd rather see them see each other as friends, equals—and, yes, gentlemen.

As to the word you used, "exclusively," no. They might on occasion do a complete turnabout, for variety's sake, or each might have to "go out" in order to satisfy the "not" part of their "more-than-not" role.

Do they tell one another that they have been "out"?

A wise gay lover keeps his own counsel. Gay love affairs with the best chance of enduring are those in which each partner realizes that his lover fulfills *most* of his sexual needs. By a conscious act of will he suppresses his lesser needs, and though he may be in part unfulfilled, he learns he can live with it.

Is it true that a mature homosexual *does not always want to play a more-than-not dominant* role?

That's so. A mature gay person may seek younger men, and if he is more-than-not submissive, he will be *submissive* with those younger partners. This kind of homosexual—and he is frequent on the scene and I consider his needs legitimate for him—usually requires a rough boy to submit to. It can be dangerous. Though mature, if he is clumsy or drunk/rude, trouble starts. If, however, age and experience have taught him that submit he must in order to function psychologically, then he has got to learn how to do it efficiently, which means—in reference to the rough boys he seeks—with fairness above all. If he has promised to pay, he must pay exactly.

What does he do sexually with such rough boys?

I will cover what homosexuals do in bed in the next chapter. He fellates them and/or they penetrate him anally.

If a mature homosexual is more-than-not dominant, can he find young boys who will submit?

In abundance. The myth that the older homosexual, fifty, sixty, is "left out" is a myth purely. If he has done anything constructive with his life, he can find young lovers who need what he has to offer. In certain places, such more-than-not dominant older men command the field.

But isn't that always a cash arrangement?

It is not always a cash arrangement. Boys exist who are erotically aroused—for whatever reason—by older men. If an older man has knowledge of some field to share, and the boy is vitally interested, that knowledge may be the boy's chief goal, but why not? It is as much a part of the older homosexual as any other part of him. Ditto, the fact of cash. There are few older/younger men arrangements that last long based only on cash. It may appear that way to an onlooker, and the boy may indeed be kept well, but it cannot last between them without other intermeshing characteristics which enhance both lives. Of course, there are hustler/older men duos but that is another subject, which I will cover in Chapter 12.

I think an interesting corollary to the older man/younger partnership is the subject of younger men who absolutely chase older men; deliberately seduce them. The older man, in that sense, is by far not the aggressor. This goes double for extremely young boys—twelve, eleven—who set their cap with sex aforethought for an older man they like and who is available to them. Parents who believe it is always the older man's "fault" when their son is deflowered and they discover it, take note.

In a gay love relationship, how can one tell which is the more-than-not dominant partner and which is the more-than-not submissive one?

For straight people, this seems to be the ultimate guessing game. The answer is, you can't—even gay people can't with absolute certainty make a judgment. What happens between two gay partners in bed may be different from the "looks of things" on the surface. The more-than-not dominant partner in bed may indeed be the shy and retiring partner out of bed. And the leader out of bed—bold, outspoken, deep-voiced —may indeed be the more-than-not submissive partner in bed.

I'm going to make one more distinction here which I hope will help you in understanding the phenomenon of gay role-playing. And this distinction is not limited to people in gay life.

Between two gay lovers, there is usually one who might be called the "mana" personality. He is the giver, the healer, the one who best solves life's constant conflict of opposites. His partner finds it stimulating and comforting to be in his presence, quite apart from what they do in bed.

Now *either* the more-than-not dominant or the more-than-not submissive partner may possess this curious quality, and that quality in him is clear to anyone, gay or straight, who takes the trouble to observe the lovers over any period of time. I will get to how the lovers exchange this quality in a symbolic sense in bed in the next chapter. Here, I would like just to mention it so that you do not confuse this healing and comforting personality trait as a necessarily feminine characteristic and think erroneously that by identifying it you have correctly identified the more-than-not submissive partner. Bluntly, the swishiest queen can have it; the roughest piece of trade can have it. Like an orchid in the jungle, "mana" is rootless and can avail itself of any type of personality.

And then, to make matters more complicated (I warned you), this "mana" quality may be deliberately concealed, visible only to a partner—but I assure you, it is there. Most of the time the "mana" personality is evident, but, as I said, it is *not* indicative of who does what to whom in bed.

But surely there must be visible signs of what role a person wants or likes to play which he offers someone he is cruising?

You'd think so, wouldn't you; it stands to reason. . . . I have urged gay people in my writing to eliminate fooling around and by saying so directly tell the potential partner while they are both still in the bar (or wherever) what is expected of one another in bed. But it isn't done, not often, except by the daring or the dauntless or the foolish. It seems to be part of the game to remain expert at revealing what one wants from a partner, and what one desires or is willing to give, while at the same time remaining ambiguous and uncommitted—I suppose, in case one is rebuffed. Gay life is also a trip up a thousand blind alleys. But these things are difficult to say for most gay people, what they *want* especially, because so much of the time they don't know, refuse to make the obvious self-inquiries, prefer on occasion not to know, but to be swept up (they hope), to play either role, by the partner of their dreams: all by purest chance! The crazy thing is that in gay life such unions occur.

Older gay people do, of course, have a system of references or quasi-leading questions to establish what it is they're after from a potential bed partner, but even these can be equivocal, short of grabbing someone's derriere lustfully, or his genitals by a grope. Either one of those gestures makes the picture clear.

You may have heard or read that in sadist-masochist bars, the wearing of a set of keys on a certain side of one's belt, or allowing a certain color handkerchief to drape just so out of the left or right rear dungaree pocket, signifies certain sexual desires. Maybe, in *one particular bar* such signals have been codified. But even those signals vary from bar to bar, not to mention place to place. And if such simple signals vary, you can imagine how the artifices of conversation with a potential bedpartner must vary as to approximately what each is looking for if indeed both or either has any real idea!

A friend has suggested to me that one must never tell,

beforehand, what one wants to do, or have done to him sexually. And I admit that the question "What do you like to do?" has been put to me and often, but not always, turned me off. This friend says that such preplanning may be possible in the area of heterosexual parenthood, but that it kills a gay sex experience out of hand—there must be mystery! He is positively annoyed that straight people know as much as they do about gay life—Must every secret be revealed? he pleads.

I do not think every secret can be revealed because so much is unknown about homosexuality, especially to homosexuals. But I think somebody, me, ought to take a shot at making sense of it for our own sakes, and for the sake of uniting in common humanity the gay and straight sensibilities.

What about *you*; how do *you* make clear what you want, one way or the other, from a potential bed partner?

I was afraid you'd ask that, and I would be compelled to think it through in order to answer you.

It is a matter for me, I think, of projecting a certain "intensity" which should give my partner an idea of what I expect —if he is receptive to that intensity in the first place. If he is receptive, then he will project back an answering current, and naturally and casually there is a touching of hands, then a caress, and perhaps even, in a gay place, a kiss. A dance together. Another kiss, and the bargain is usually sealed: I can tell from a kiss, I guess anyone can, who is going to do, more or less, what to whom. But I have been mistaken, too. You see, anything can happen to disrupt a pair of gay people who have established rapport, right up until the moment they actually get in bed. Only then—after a few minutes—can one tell whether or not the affair is going to work out. At least, for that one time. Lovers are the lucky ones, of course, who "get it together" more than once, who somehow jump the hurdles standing in the way of a relationship, and there are a good many of those, and yet manage to "keep it together." A complete and enduring love affair in gay life is almost as much of a miracle as the entry into a woman's vagina of that one spermatozoon that fertilizes her womb. Both events do occur —but at what cost of elimination of possibilities!

I have learned several things about cruising—for me.

First, I try to ascertain in my mind in advance what role would fulfill me that particular night (it may be the opposite one tomorrow night though I do have a more-than-not preference), and I sally forth, as it were, seeking, in appearance at least, the partner who would fulfill me. Now if I am in the mood to be more-than-not submissive (it happens), I go to a bar where a more rugged crowd hangs out. If the opposite desire is uppermost, I go to a dance bar where a younger, less experienced crowd hangs out. That decision, and my consequent role that evening, is at least established in form, if not content. Chance favors the prepared mind.

Then, I have learned to wait and watch—as nearly everybody else is doing, even if they're dancing wildly. Wait and watch for someone to take more than a lingering look in my direction. Meanwhile, I am taking more than a lingering look in someone else's direction. It is best for me in a bar to wait for someone to pick me out. (That's what everybody thinks!) It does work for me if I can keep my sense of myself. There's the rub, and it is the rub for most gay people. A while standing around or dancing around a noisy bar and all traces of that "intensity" I mentioned begin to drain out of me; it depends upon how strong I feel that evening or how severe that old must-be-satisfied need is. I know, however, when it is gone and I am straining, or I am flat out of it—time to go home. Even if the most ravishing image of my desire should walk in (everybody watches a gay bar door) I would be helpless to approach him, or even to project in eyeball-to-eyeball contact that necessary "intensity." I know that others have the same experience. In gay life—that dear phrase—quite frequently, eyeball-to-eyeball contact turns the trick, but I still must feel up to it. If I am up to it, and a person approaches who is a reasonable facsimile of my desire, I take it: I have at least learned not to be too choosy.

What is communicated between gay people in that strictly eyeball-to-eyeball contact?

The same thing that is always communicated in such a contact. ("Let your soul be in your eyes.") Theater, movies, TV, and novels are redolent with such moments—in gay life an initial agreement of prima facie mutual attractiveness—but as many conversations as are begun after such contact, I suspect as many languish after a few minutes. The S & M people claim that an S can spot an M, and without a word walk with him, go to his place, carry on as S & M people are wont to do, both playing their roles to perfection, and then exit, with meaningful looks. It has never happened to me. (More about S & M in Chapter 11.)

In all this talk about roles, isn't there an element of playacting?

You are right, there is. But the playacting is simply to point up, to dramatize, *the needs that exist*. A more-than-not dominant gay person knows what his more-than-not submissive partner needs, dominance in bed, and if he does not supply it, he is not going to facilitate the kind of sex both of them like. The submissive partner, by the way, usually initiates the action, and delimits it.

Playacting—yes! Labels—absolutely! It is important to keep in mind that *the labels did not invent the roles,* the roles spring from a very deep human need in homosexuals to dominate or to submit in the course of sexual activity. The young, as I say, dispute this, until they get in bed with someone they conceived in their illusion to be a "Man" and he disappoints by turning out to be someone as much in need of domination as they are at that moment.

Why do you have reservations about gay role-playing out of bed?

It doesn't work. I admit, however, that it is necessary *sometimes* for the self-esteem of the "dominant" partner—as well as for the fulfillment of the "submissive" partner—that the dominant partner *never* relinquish his role. He must in all situations in life in which they are mutual participants be in command. This means that between two lovers, the "dominant" partner must usually have more money at his disposal, be determined to initiate any action in and out of bed, and generally behave like a breast-beating male.

But I thought you said Mommy and Daddy were not the role-playing models for homosexuals?

I maintain it. If there is any model for gay role-playing, it is the *typical struggle between two males for supremacy*. When it works, the two of them seem to thrive on the conflict: one always strong, the other always defeated, if not outright humiliated. From the outside, it looks awful, but how the two of them adore it, and when they get to bed, how marvelously in each other's eyes all the proofs of either role reward their sexual activity.

Have you involved yourself in the male-supremacy struggle out of bed?

I have, and I can report there is ecstasy along with complete exhaustion. At first, when I was young, I sought a "Man." I was a victim of that illusion harbored by both gay and straight. Once in a while, I thought I'd found what I was looking for —namely in Key West during the great days of the naval post there—but I was soon painfully aware that I was seeking a phantom that existed only in popular song lyrics. I learned: *There is no such thing as a "Man."* There are big, bulky boys who might throw a hard punch in a bar scrap, but when it came to infighting in the real world, the adversary arena of commerce, those bulky boys hadn't a chance. What I did discover is that there are some homosexuals who, in bed, are reasonably mentally equipped to play a dominant role, but even then, one must not expect too much, or even a consistent performance. Therefore my phrase "more-than-not," which you may be tired of reading but which acquires significance in this context. In bed with bulky boys, one satisfies mostly illusion.

This works in reverse, too. *Boys are not girls*. I have had love affairs in which I carried the more-than-not dominant role, and I made the mistake (often) of treating my "submissive" partner like a girl, which is the way he seemed to want it, especially in bed. I was wrong: He may have been more-than-not submissive in bed, but several months of being treated like a girl in and out of bed built up in him a tidal wave of anger, which periodically overflowed in my direction, and finally sunk us.

I am outlining to you now some of the conundrums of homosexual love. These things exist; these relationships are ongoing right this minute. And so you can understand that there is a lot of infidelity and promiscuity in gay life *because love relationships aren't easy*. If more could be learned about the dynamics of homosexual love, we gay people might have a chance; it's not mostly society's opposition to homosexuality that makes things so difficult (although that often worsens the matter); *it's that as gay people we know so little about ourselves in love*. But I understand that the heterosexual world is in the same predicament. In answer to your question, yes, I have played the male supremacy game, both major roles, in and out of bed. It is the only game in town, objections from young mishmash lovers notwithstanding.

Is it to be inferred that there is a certain amount of illusion necessary for homosexual lovemaking that concretizes in the more-than-not roles which are played?

Yes, good gay sex is predicated on the necessary, artful illusion of role-playing. But I think if we can get hold of this idea of "necessary!" illusion *in bed, and not carry it out of bed*—expect unreal behavior in one role direction or the other—then we have made a start toward the constructive manipulation of illusion, rather than being manipulated by illusion. We must do something, grab hold and get control somehow of the morass of psychological projection and counterprojection that characterizes a gay love relationship. These projections are going to continue; there must be a method of stabilizing them. That is our problem with role-playing.

How does role-playing resolve itself among homosexuals in prison?

No frills. The dominant partner is King Kong and the submissive partner is Fay Wray, without the screams.

Chapter 4

What Homosexuals Do in Bed

How can a male really be attracted emotionally and erotically to another male?

I can understand your difficulty in imagining this, if you have never seen or minutely inwardly experienced it, but it happens. As I've emphasized, it does *not* happen in the way Dr. Rubin gave you to believe. It is not a matter of wanting to become a woman, or being ardently desirous of penis entry somewhere, somehow, into another male's body. That kind of approach to the subject is nonsense. There is emotional attraction, there is aesthetic preference, an appreciation of beauty of the entire male physique—or maybe only the face, or even just the eyes. And beyond all that or perhaps as the sum of it, there is *love* among gay people. There is even love—as severely as you may define it—in the actions of two gay people who are together for only an hour: more passion and ecstasy between them than some people know in a lifetime. Oh yes, a male can love a male and does. He loves everything about him: where he lives, what he wears, how he speaks, and of course, how he looks. Not only that, but there is an intensity about the entire erotic attraction matched only by the intense loneliness of gay lovers when they are separated. Homosexual loneliness for a lover who has been lost is responsible for a good deal of literature, theater, and music. It has got to be expressed or it will kill.

Is this chapter going to tell us things that are stomach-turning?

There is no sexual practice described in this chapter that you have not come across in any heterosexual sex manual: oral penetration, anal penetration, and mutual masturbation are familiar standbys. Fist penetration may be new-ish. (Human copulating positions are not known for their dignity.)

Don't gay men want to be women?

No, no, and no. That is Rubin speaking through you again. Gay men are men and proud of it; most gay people these days are well turned out physically. Straight people can and have taken a leaf from their book when it comes to a full realization of the potential of the male physique. *Repeat:* male and proud of it.

Don't transsexuals and transvestites and drag queens want to be women?

We've been over this before, but let's take it again. Transsexuals; yes. Transvestites; in appearance only. Drag queens; for the hell of it, but not permanently.

But isn't that sort of thing outright masochism?

Rubin stressed and titillated his readers with what he made of gay life as a masochistic enterprise. You were "had" by his simplistic and pejorative generalizations, injuriously misinformed. I have in detail corrected your impression of *transsexuals*: powerful individualists who with the courage of their convictions transform themselves into women; a special

66

experience that has little to do with homosexuality. *Transvestites:* mostly heterosexual males who have taken the veil of Isis and, like Ulysses in peril, feel safe and happy wearing women's apparel—connection with the mother-image, etc., a phenomenon of fetishism, only bordering on homosexuality. *Drag queens* dress like women or throw on an old boa or bugle-beaded gown and it isn't even parody anymore—it's just for the fun of the thing! They are usually homosexuals with amusing flair: the best of them are female impressionists, maybe twenty of note in the country, whose art is a venerable and respected one. None of those things is masochistic in nature, and only one is distinctly homosexual.

A conceptual jumble of these three separate types, coated with fear, superstition, and distortion of the facts—is, regrettably, the usual content of a mother's idea of her son as homosexual.

Is it really true that a male can get an erection looking at another male?

This is exactly the same question, rephrased, that you asked at the start of this chapter, and no matter how many times you ask it, I am willing to answer it, and I can understand your amazement. Yes, it is true—an erection by looking at another male, and holding him and kissing him and getting undressed with him and getting in bed with him and having sex —without any thought of anything but each other, immersed in each other's concupiscence. And happy that they are both males, but aware as the particular sexual experience progresses that a certain amount of dominant-submissive role-playing is going to take place that will drive them both to ecstasy.

But isn't that another way of saying that one of the two lovers is playing the female role?

No—the process is different, the results are different! And incidentally, the idea of equating the submissive homosexual role to a woman's role in bed is a slap to women. In bed, homosexuals *are* submissive (if that is their more-than-not role), and to my way of thinking that behavior works, is psychologically healthy. But a woman who is expected in bed to be submissive simply because she's a woman and that is a woman's predestined role is being insulted and put upon before the sexual act is even begun!

What do homosexuals do in bed?

Ah, I thought you'd never ask! Physically, and here again, this is a "construct" model—emphasized, exaggerated, or even minimized, in order that you may have a picture—*generally*—of what does go on. It might be difficult, except at the moment of orgasm—when there is no doubt—to see the "action" clearly if you witnessed the lovers making love, and to say definitely at any point—ah, there is the "submissive stance" or "69" or whatever. But, schematically —and with role-playing an uppermost consideration—here's what happens:

69: perhaps the most famous and venerable homosexual sexual stance. The lovers—and we will for the sake of graphics consider our observed participants as lovers—lie feet to head, feet to head, and move up slightly, usually lying on their sides, and they suck each other's penis. When lovers are in the stage of their sexual lives when mutuality is de rigueur, 69 is the fairest way to proceed. Sometimes the orgasm can be simultaneous, and of course, then it is best. I think you will find that gay people do *not* mostly anymore care for 69. It is damnably uncomfortable for most gays, who must do acrobatics to maintain their mouths (or penises) in place, or who must be masters at split attention to enjoy their own act of sucking, the while being performed upon below and attempting to extract full enjoyment from that. As I said, for lovers bent upon mutuality —which as role-playing is as binding as any other kind—it is satisfying. I can't hack 69 physically anymore, nor does it gratify me or my partners in terms of our roles.

Oral penetration: One person sucks the other's penis, and is masturbated by him, or masturbates himself. Although active with his body and mouth in the extreme, the sucking partner is performing the more-than-not submissive role, and in his mind he is enjoying the performance of that role; utterly, at that moment, submissive and receiving of his lover whom he adores. Meanwhile, the suckee is enjoying the physical sensations of his partner's moist, hot mouth teasing and surrounding and sucking his penis. As the more-than-not dominant partner, he is also enjoying, in his mind, his feeling that he is master of the world. If you as a male have never had a pretty gay boy fellate you, you've missed an experience that certain heterosex sex manuals recommend as a warm-up for straight sex. Or, if you, as a woman, have never had a gay boy perform upon you the act of cunnilingus, or performed fellatio on him, you too have missed an experience. But I mustn't be carried away. . . .

Incidentally, I will speak of the symbolic exchange of my concept of "mana" between lovers in a moment.

Anal penetration is the second main type of homosexual sex. Some gays would put it in first place, and indulge in it exclusively.

It can be accomplished with the lovers lying down on their sides, back to front, or one on top of the other, or one with his legs in the air, or one sitting on top of the other. All these positions are familiar heterosexual stances.

While the lover who is penetrating the anus is doing so, he reaches around and masturbates his partner. Sometimes the anal stimulation of the partner being penetrated is so great that, via the prostate gland massage he receives en passant, he comes without masturbatory assistance.

In anal penetration, as in oral penetration, who does what to whom is governed by the more-than-not roles the lovers are playing. The one who is being penetrated is, of course, the more-than-not submissive partner—at least on this occasion—and the other partner is the more-than-not dominant. This act, as well as the act of oral penetration, is often accompanied by the particular language of adoration, "Shove it in deep, master," or the language of humiliation, "Take it, you bitch"—all proper in bed, to be dismissed out of bed by both partners.

There is no act of homosexual sex that is unfamiliar (in form) to the readers of routine heterosexual sex manuals. Or to heterosexual sex jocks.

Isn't there anything new and different?

Aside from S & M practices, which are faddish now, and which I'll cover in Chapter 11, the answer is, not really.

Maybe fist penetration—the whole fist and wrist and sometimes forearm is thrust into the anus. It's mostly an S & M "thing." But it can be done between ordinary gay dominant-submissive lovers (the more-than-not submissive partner receives the fist) not as an act of dominant enslavement but as a *curious act of love* in that the fist entry signifies a passion to grasp the vitals, the very soul of the partner being penetrated. If you try it, use plenty of lubricant.

But don't gay people lament the absence of a vagina?

I have never missed it. The human physique offers at least two other convenient apertures, both "officially" zoned as erogenous, and those apertures do fine.

Are there other homosexual sex practices?

Mutual masturbation, which Dr. Rubin ranks first, is usually the last resort between two lovers, or something that they do to vary their sexual activity. Doing it in front of a mirror is amusing, and gives the participants the effect of third party voyeurs. If it is done with finesse and, of course, with love, it can be gratifying. Mutual masturbation is practiced frequently by gay people who've just met and who have yet to determine between them who is going to play which role really. I have never known a love relationship to last between gay people who relied only on mutual masturbation. There has got to be greater sexual rapport. If they care for one another enough, they find a way.

But isn't the anus the repository of feces?

Gay people learn to clear their anuses; most have healthy systems, regular evacuations—I can honestly say I have not run into difficulty with this. If a gay person cannot clear his anus naturally before being penetrated, there are douches, exact duplicates of vaginal douches.

What are some of the fetishistic sex practices of gays?

Analingus, of course—good for the facial muscles, many gay people aver. A "candy-ass" boy is delightful.

There is dildo anal-penetration, and then there's *mutual* anal penetration: accomplished with a two-foot length of plastic hose, contoured on both ends with the simulated glans of a penis. Each of the lovers inserts one end of the gadget into his own anus and (rear to rear) they rock back and forth. The effect, presumably, is of each penetrating the other—a synthetic method, and not convincing.

Lovers have their own "specialties": tonguing nipples, or belly buttons, or kneecaps, or toes—as well as longish, high-flown licking and teasing of the genitalia area and the genitalia.

Anything else?

Electric-powered gadgetry for masturbatory purposes is in vogue, although I believe gay people send for the things, try 'em once, and then give them away as fun gifts at parties. Porn movies are getting better and better (story line and scenery): excellent as starter-uppers for orgies, intimate or grand.

Are gay people as really orgy-minded as they seem?

Yes, "for them that likes it" orgies are popular. If, truly, a lover or a love affair is not on one's mind, gay people have the capacity for adoration of flesh, heaps and heaps of gorgeous flesh, that is awe-inspiring. They certainly have restored "the body" to its rightfully important place in human affairs. In our age, busy people (concerned with money and matters of consequence) tend to conceive of themselves as having heads only, with little wings attached. Gay people set a good example for such people in their love of arms and legs and necks and pectoral muscles and shapely rears and curvacious thighs—their own and others commingled and rubbing and pumping away in a joyous orgy!

71

Is a large penis a pressing consideration among gay people?

Doubtless, for some—an irresistible symbol of greater than average sexual libido. I believe it carries the same connotations in the heterosexual world. There are gay people whom a large penis fascinates in itself; but again, one is speaking of fetishistic minority. It is the human being with whom a gay person falls in love; love is the name of the game, always has been. I am speaking of the experience of most gay people.

But don't homosexuals go to lengths to wear pants that outline their genitals?

Fairly snug fitting clothing is "in" generally. Yes, some gay boys feel that they want to show a little "basket." I have known heterosexuals who feel similarly. At summer resorts, gay people do often wear clothes that reveal the outline of their genitalia. Back home, in the office, they wear what everybody else wears. I might add that a homosexual of any sartorial taste eschews too tight pants. And no, most homosexuals do *not* tape, strap, or otherwise artificially support their genitalia for display purposes.

I want to add this note: The seeming preoccupation of gays with genitalia is about the same thing as ostensible heterosexual preoccupation with female breasts. The preoccupation mostly takes the form of lascivious banter; a gay conversational gambit when the office clock moves slowly, or when two gays are cruising together.

It is true (and sexy if the boy is attractive) that common street hustlers publicly manipulate their penises into a half-erection in their pants in order to get attention (see Chapter 12).

How about gay people who cruise subway toilets, aren't they looking exclusively for a penis? Or a number of penises?

Gay people who deliberately and consistently cruise public toilets are candidates for a psychiatrist's couch; they need help. They do *not* represent homosexuals; this is the seamier side of a human being's desperation.

How does the concept of "mana" work into gay sex?

Either partner can be the mana personality, or it may be that both have an element of it—making them a superior pair of lovers indeed. Usually, one of them possesses it and if he is the more-than-not dominant partner, his lover enjoys sucking it out of him, along with the sperm. If the more-than-not submissive partner has it, his lover enjoys screwing it out of him. It is the quality of something "extra," which, exchanged during sex, makes the act more meaningful for both. You will find little about it in any sex manual, but it is part of gay sex—this *mind-sex* without which sex is mind*less*—and gay people know about it. So far as your homosexual sensibility is concerned, you might try out this mana concept in bed with a heterosexual partner whom you feel possesses this mysterious and fortunate "power and at-oneness with the universe." It is transferable. I suspect women will recognize and understand what I am describing here better than men. I think it is a rare male who would or does admit this mystical quality which eludes him, and he wants and women seem to have. I am being outrageous about mana, but I know how to be outrageous sometimes, and sometimes it is the only way to get a point across. Remember mana: It is the one characteristic that I would wholeheartedly agree that some women and some homosexuals share, in reference to their lovers.

Doesn't a homosexual who is more-than-not submissive in bed unman himself?

That's one of the myths, too—and, again, it has a long history. According to Thorkil Vanggaard, in his book *Phallos*, the ancient Norsemen believed just that, and had a word for it: *argr*. Says Vanggaard, "argr is the crudest form of abuse in old Norse. Applied to a man it not only implied that he was effeminate, but that he submitted himself to being used sexually as a woman." And from the same book, Vanggaard, speaking of argr and the old Norse conception of it: "To be able to mount another man is an expression of superiority and strength and rank and so is honorable, while it is a sign of weakness and submission to be forced to present and be mounted, a cause of disgrace to a man. . . ."

A man of note who felt that anal penetration (which it would seem Vanggaard is describing) was a thing of peril and shame: T. E. Lawrence, called Lawrence of Arabia. The Turks captured him on one of his expeditions and according to his biographers, they forced anal intercourse with him, and when he returned to England he felt *something* that caused him ever after to avoid public life. In a letter to a friend, he strongly implies that after what had happened to him, he felt unmanned. But I wonder about Lawrence. . . .

The answer to your question, does the more-than-not submissive partner in bed "unman himself" is no. One of my fondest memories is of an orgy that took place in the apartment of a famous literary agent. The man played the more-than-not anally submissive role for five hours in succession with at least six participants. The next day I happened to visit him in his office, and saw and heard him pursuing the course of his normal day—as direct and cold and astute about his business as the shark in *Jaws* was about its business. Unman him? His previous night's activities seemed to have loosed in him the greater power of his cunning and power-game playing: I heard him on the phone "up" a client's literary advance by $10,000 with sheer malice in his noncommittal voice.

Homosexuals do not believe that playing the more-than-not submissive role in bed unmans anyone. Sophisticated gays boast of the brilliance of their performances in bed in that role. The role has lost its "inferior" connotation because it was the myth of a guilty mind, and that sense of guilt has been proven needless and it has been shattered. The only observable physical residue of having been submissive in bed the night before is a certain soreness around the anus, which may be relieved with aspirin.

If, in the spirit of détente between us, I agree to the fact that the distinctions you have made between homosexual role-playing and heterosexual role-playing in its form and results are acceptable, *will you agree* that a submissive homosexual in bed during the sex act

shares *some* of a woman's feelings in the same situation?

Yes; I'm certain that the two do coincide at certain moments. Perhaps in the act of surrender.

Have I "gotcha"?

But a male is surrendering a male body, and taking pride in doing so. His is a "proud-humility," as Tennessee Williams remarked in another context. Whereas (at least before women's lib) a woman was expected to surrender and gave the man nothing more than his due—it was no act of choice on her part. Yes, doubtless there are similarities of pure feeling, else male novelists could never write love scenes from the woman's point of view that were convincing—and, in fact, males mostly have written the best such love scenes. I concur in part to your final question, in the growing spirit of détente between us.

Chapter 5

Theories About How It All Began

How does a male get to be homosexual?

A question much asked these days, and you are justified in posing it. As I am justified in my answer to the question: *Nobody* has come up with (1) an answer acceptable to the community of doctors of the soul or (2) one acceptable or even mildly persuasive to homosexuals. Gay people today are inclined to embrace their homosexuality early, and try to live it with good grace. Psychiatrists today have all but given up attempting to "change" homosexuals. Once in a while, they have a moderate success in readaptation of an overt homosexual to heterosexuality, but the patient must assist at this 100 percent. Usually, the patient whose libidinous interests are redirected has something important (and exclusive to the sexual situation) at stake—for instance, a high living young friend of mine who was flamboyantly homosexual, saw a psychiatrist, and apparently turned straight, and married. Bully for him, if that's what he wanted. Years later I saw him cruising in a gay bar and I asked him what had happened to his cure, not to mention his wife. "Oh," he answered between dances, "my parents made it clear they'd cut me off completely if they found out I was gay. They're dead, I've inherited the million, and I can be myself." So much for psychiatry.

What theory do gay people themselves reach for?

Gay people do not "reach" for any theory. The idea of "reaching" for a theory carries with it the suggestion that they require an explanation to themselves or to the world as to why they are what they are—and that what they are is wrong or sinful or sick. Since gay people have begun to realize that it is fun to be gay, and possible to live constructive and fulfilling lives with or without others' approval or disapproval, they are too busy actualizing their own thoughts and feelings to worry about first causes. "Gay is," as we discussed in an earlier chapter.

Straight people who "reach" for theories are obviously those who need a theory to absolve themselves of imagined responsibility, or to justify their homophobia, or because they feel they missed the boat by *not* becoming gay, and would like to know how to do it!

But isn't homosexuality a sickness, really?

No, really it is not, as Dr. Kinsey tried to communicate. But the time was not right for him to say directly what he tried to imply: that 20 million people in America were exclusively or partly gay, albeit undercover, and they seemed to him not sick, but reasonably well adjusted! I believe Dr. Kinsey would be gratified by the phenomenon of homosexuality today: its openness, its lovingness, its effectiveness as a clear-cut life-style. If you read him closely, there is a faint appeal for the validity of homosexuality in his famous sexual study. Sick? No! As Dr. Thomas S. Szasz advised in his book *The Manufacture of Madness*, the "sickness" theory is merely an updating of the old "sin" theory, except that the "product" (of homosexuality) has been converted from heresy to illness.

The sickness theory (I'll get back to the sin theory) is predicated on a too-close relationship to the mother and/or to a father who was weak, absent, or indifferent. There's an auxiliary clause: If you had a brother or even a sister with whom you felt a rivalry and to whom you usually lost, you became gay. Would that it were that easy! No, as gay people began to pour out of the closets and tell their stories, *happy* gay people, some of them had the prescribed family atmosphere for homosexuality, some of them hated their mothers and adored their fathers, some loved both, hated both, or loved and hated both, had sisters and brothers whom they strong-armed or assisted—and finally the sickness theory foundered like the unseaworthy *Titanic*, and it slipped silently beneath the swells of a starlit sea of contradiction. Like the ship, the sickness theory couldn't hold water.

What about the sin theory?

I rather like the sin theory. It amuses me. The "curse from on high" crowd held sway for years, backed by biblical authority. What amused me about it was that *parents* were so attracted to it. It was *their* sin that the poor child had inherited. Those wild activities of *theirs* were to blame; the piper had now to be paid in terms of a gay son or lesbian daughter. But what fun the parents had recalling their mad experiences in youth that resulted in this catastrophe visited upon the next generation. Woe! Woe! *Mea culpa*—much churchgoing and priestly consultation as to how to expiate those delicious sins of the past and exonerate their offspring. Regrettably, some of those "curse from on high" crowd turned their kids away, refused contact, or incarcerated them in private schools cum mental institutions —and sadly, the kids believed it and accepted the punishment of rejection, insulin, or electric-shock treatments. The parents' guilt was successfully internalized in the gay child and he suffered.

Just as I enjoyed the moment in the movie *I'll Cry Tomorrow* when Lillian Roth's hand was shown reaching for her first drink (gin, I think, offered by a nurse as a mild sedative), I would love to have been there when the first gay boy—it must have happened somewhere—said to his parents, "But Dad, Mother, I don't feel sick 'cause I'm gay. I like it!" The repercussions of that brave lad's statement are still repercussing. I should imagine his parents perished in pillars of flame on the spot.

The sin theory as the cause of homosexuality is a verdict —as modern court judges say when they nullify or reverse a jury's guilty finding—that has been "set aside."

How about the "security disease" theory?

That is a theory not many people know has been promulgated. At first glance, I thought it might have merit. It contends that because of weakness or fault of mind or bodily constitution, homosexuality develops in a lad because he seeks someone strong to fend for him in the world and he confuses this need for a hero-protector-provider, with love, if an approximation (with muscles) of such a person can be found.

It certainly seemed an observable fact that many gay people were financially naïve. They couldn't "find their way across town," as the gay expression goes, much less earn their keep at a real job. It hadn't occurred to me when I gave some credence to the security disease theory that maybe specific discrimination against gay people in the commercial arena worked objectively against them and instilled their ignorance.

Now gay people are around and about in the commercial world. Businessmen have discovered it is disadvantageous to their product or service to take an antihomosexual attitude: It's not nice to fool around with Mother Nature *or gay people;* unspoken gay solidarity against a business's product or service results in a chartable drop in sales figures.

The security disease theory is *out.* Dizzy-queen members of our clan are doing fine financially these days, thank you—as well as being the recipients, as I've mentioned, of acclaim from gay libbers as having been among the first to defy the world and proclaim their gay individuality. In fact, one platinum blond young friend of mine, in banking, realized a decent sum from his Wall Street flutter, and he's bought a house in the Hamptons and he gets there from his East Side New York brownstone in his new Jaguar XJ convertible. If, indeed, homosexuality resulted from some sort of financial incapacity, I am glad to report that the disease has been eradicated. And happily, homosexuality continues to flourish.

What about the "inborn psychic masochist" theory?

Oh yes, the gist of that one was that gay people enjoyed suffering to the extent that they promoted situations in life (indeed became gay), just so they could suffer more horribly. That theory reeks of the psychiatrist's couch. Gay people who consulted the soul doctors in the old days must have seemed to the doctors perverse individuals who obviously insisted upon the acting-out of desires that any sensible person put down early on, and this acting-out got them in trouble, if not with the law, then by arousing their own guilt feelings which eventuated in a constant state of depression. Poor fools, the doctors must have thought, to subject themselves to such conditions: Why, of course, they must enjoy it, be gratified by it; they suffer because they are homosexual and they remain masochistically inclined to suffer because pain to them is pleasure—and proper retribution, incidentally, for being so perverse as to want to continue to be homosexual. If I lost you on that last roundabout of reasoning, so did the doctors lose their patients when the patients learned to *stop* feeling guilty, and *go* with their homosexuality. Now that the world has practically put out a sign (not SE HABLA ESPAÑOL, but HOMOSEXUALS WELCOME HERE), the type of gay person who used to look to soul doctors as if he liked to suffer, suffers no more.

S & M (which I shall cover in Chapter 11), involves suffering but the desire of the masochist partner for pain is different, and fun-filled.

We are but partway through the chapter on how it all began, and it is amazing, I should think to you as well as to me, what hogwash gay people have had thrown at them through the years. A modern gay person's sensibility, and the gay part of it we are evoking out of your present sensibility, has been achieved only by those early gay pilgrims wading, and sometimes drowning, in rivers of merde.

Does the "nature's birth control" theory go down too?

I rather like that theory: to be, as a homosexual, a part of nature's predestined "grand plan" for the survival of the human race. It has a majesty about it. It gives gay people a key position in the eminent scheme of things, makes them a "chosen" minority, whereas, heretofore, we had been a disdained minority. But I'm afraid it would be inexcusable hubris on our parts to hope for such munificence from on high instead of the curse that we had been led to expect existed. It's going from one extreme to the other, and as we all know, extremities are to be avoided, especially when the presumed author is God. No, us gays can't claim it (and then it seems a contraindication of Mother Nature's birth control theory when she allowed poor old Oscar Wilde to father two healthy children!).

Wasn't there talk about homosexuality as a concomitant of genius?

If there wasn't, there should have been, for the world knows that all people of genius are homosexual, *ergo*, all homosexuals are geniuses. And if you believe that one, let me tell you about the frog that turned into a prince. . . .

How about the "genetic predisposition" theory?

Dr. Money testified at length on this old saw at the trial of the aforementioned Sergeant Matlovitch. The theory asserts that Dad gave Mom too many of those spirally things of the wrong gender during impregnation, or . . . was it that Mom should have conceived a girl but mistakenly birthed a boy, or . . . I don't quite remember. Whatever, this theory attributes homosexuality to a chemical process that went off course somewhere before a homosexual was born, therefore inevitably predisposing him to that sexual orientation. It is a slyly deprecating idea. It removes the responsibility for his homosexuality from the homosexual's domain of *choice*. It *denies* that, responding to homosexual promptings as well as heterosexual promptings (as we all do), he *consciously chose to be homosexual*. The subtle undermining involved here is incredulousness and disbelief that anyone would prefer to be gay—as if that were the worst alternative anyone could imagine! Surely (the reasoning of the geneticists goes) homosexuals are led to such a choice by factors beyond their control. To which most homosexuals—whatever the validity or invalidity of the theory—would answer with a vulgar word or gesture that I shall simply render as: nuts to genetic predisposition. And I think that that opinion is the prevalent one.

Is the theory of a woman's-brain-in-a-man's-body viable?

For transsexuals, yes. For most gay people, I think not. Certainly not for me. But I do recognize that psychic mysteries exist. I recognize transsexuality as one of the most profound. I also recognize the profound mystery of the lives of the saints who have experienced a union with God. Transsexuals have much in common with the saints. And that is as far as I dare go.

Is it true that men become homosexual because they fear women?

You mean they fear psychological castration in the company of women, or they fear the responsibility involved if they got married and had to perform as breadwinner out of bed and superman in bed. Therefore, they eschew the company of women, much less a formal relationship, and turn homosexual. I think that theory rests on the slimmest of premises. Many homosexuals marry and have children. Many homosexuals are devoted to the needs of women—hairdressers, clothing designers, interior decorators—and have lengthy professional and personal relationships with women. Many homosexuals cherish a particular woman friend as confidante and adviser. Women have led the way, and gay people have willingly followed, in the matter of "liberation." Women who for years have been "liberated" (defiantly themselves), like Bette Davis, Mae West, Hepburn, Dietrich, Garbo, have long been idolized by gays for their individuality.

I don't believe homosexuals fear women will castrate them or shy away from the problems of a formal relationship because they are not able to face responsibility. I believe—and this leads us to the next theory, my own—*that an erotic-aesthetic preference for men supersedes a homosexual's erotic interest, if any, in the female sex*—just that and nothing more or less than that. Unless a homosexual is dreadfully discontent with his homosexuality (it happens), I see no point in forcing upon him a different erotic-aesthetic preference (as the soul doctors do by what they call "aversion therapy," via the use of drugs causing a gay person to vomit at the sight of a picture of male genitals, etc.). A gay person's preference for the male body is not an insult to the beauty of women (which gay people serve with their crafts to reinforce); it is a different taste; an element of which exists in everyone's psyche, and which homosexuals have chosen to express, to actualize in their experience, and which fulfills them.

But if a homosexual could be maneuvered into having a good lay with a woman, wouldn't he want to change?

Yes, that is a natural thought. First, I suspect that there are few exclusively homosexual people. Most homosexuals, like most heterosexuals in relation to homosexual experience, have probably had a go at "it" some time in their lives. But if they're persistently gay, then we can surmise that heterosexuality didn't "take," just as early homosexual experience that heterosexuals have doesn't "take." You can't make a person dislike oranges by causing him to enjoy prunes. I mean no disrespectful comparison, of course. No, the mere fact of a satisfactory orgasm with a woman, even a stupendously satisfactory orgasm, is not going to change our Little Boy Blue into the wolf-man, however well intended the experiment may be. Many have tried, but few homosexuals stick around long enough to try again—even if their heterosexual sex is successful. It is not dislike of women. It is preferring success in another mode.

What is your theory of homosexuality?

I call it the aesthetic theory—which only means that there are men who respond to other men as *beautiful*, as proper conduits for them of their esteem, adoration, erotic-arousal, and love.

Is that an unusual theory?

I am amazed at how rarely *pure aesthetic preference* is mentioned in regard to homosexuality. That a male, to whatever degree androgynous, could please the eye with the contours of his physique, the ear with the sound of his voice, the senses of touch, taste, and smell with whatever the male offers to gratify those senses—that this aesthetic preference, and this alone, could be the cause, the substance, and the purpose of homosexuality seems hardly ever given serious consideration. For me, the beauty of my lover, *as I see it*, is paramount for me. Others may not agree that in an objective judgment he is even particularly attractive, but to me, he is beautiful. Such aesthetic senses as I possess, and their degree of sensitivity, are fulfilled when I behold him, when I hear him, touch him, taste him, and smell him. I love him, to me he is *beautiful*—and the fulfillment of that aesthetic ideal has ever been the motivation for my homosexuality. I am proud to say that I have fulfilled it, more than once.

Are there other major theories?

No, that about wraps it up.

What can I conclude?

It may be that for some homosexuals, at some periods in their lives, in some places, in some degree, these theories or parts of several explain their homosexuality. I wish you would conclude from this chapter what most homosexuals conclude: The origin of homosexuality is *unknowable*. What is knowable, what is important is that *they exist as homosexuals in the world, right now, this minute*—and the thing to do is to live their lives as wisely, responsibly, and as lovingly as they can.

Chapter 6

"Coming Out" These Days

Is a distinction to be made between a gay person's "coming out" these days as opposed to times past?

Yes. In times past, about the best a person could do who had discovered his homosexuality consciously was to acknowledge it to himself. He took his (future) life in his hands if he dared to acknowledge it publicly, and most parents reacted violently to such an admission.

And what is the situation now?

It is better, though not ideal. If your son or daughter—yes, yours!—comes to you with such an admission, you are probably sufficiently informed not to receive the news with the kind of utter revulsion that used to be standard.

You have heard of homosexuality—there have been extensive newspaper and TV news reports. Homosexual characters in TV variety shows are mandatory it would seem: Cher gets off a gay remark, Mary Tyler Moore says quite casually "He's gay," and one of America's most popular comics has simply transferred his acidulous voice and comments from his private life to his TV appearances, and the whole country laughs with him. Television handles homosexuality gingerly but it is definitely not under the kind of severe media suppression as had been the case ten years ago. TV writers depend upon general "recognition" of a gay character and the lingo doesn't go over your head anymore. And I shouldn't think if you discovered or were told that a relative, friend, or business associate was gay, you'd faint. Or hit him. Or throw up. Those were not uncommon past reactions. In fact, if you are following along here with me in *Straight Answers*, as to evoking in yourself a homosexual sensibility, the original process of coming out by someone you know, or are in touch with, can be particularly instructive. I will come back to this.

How is "coming out" accomplished?

It is rarely a clear-cut move. It is so nebulous sometimes to the person who is coming out that other people may suspect it before he himself does. It begins to dawn on a gay person usually when he experiences a severe attraction to someone of his own sex—and that attraction can consist of just wanting to be near a "friend." In the company of this "friend" the potentially gay individual feels exultation, or peace, or brightness; good feelings mainly. Ah, but when they are separated, the nascent gay sensibility is dark and brooding, and woefully involved in keeping track of the friend's activities in actuality or imagination. Proust's entire *Swann's Way* portrayed such an attachment.

Is "coming out" ever quick?

It can be as immediately manifest as a religious conversion, and in a sense as natural. Nevertheless it has been long in preparation in the unconscious of the potentially overt gay person. And then, on higher levels of awareness, a gay person may suddenly realize that the funny things he's been doing with certain friends in a half-conscious state *is* homosexuality, and that "homosexual" is the word to describe his primary sexual orientation. He comes out quickly, it is a relief for such a gay person to understand at last, and consciously assimilate, the exact nature of a compulsion that seemed to rob him of his self-control when it held him in thrall: cruising johns or parks in a half-dazed state.

What about men who "come out" late in life?

It must be devastating to an intelligent man to acknowledge to himself that he has lived in a miasma of self-deception regarding his homosexuality. That he has married, spawned children (whom he may certainly love and care for), established a home and a circle of friends—but more in response to what he felt he *should be* rather than in response to what he finds he truly *is*. Such men sometimes go hog-wild when they finally come out—they are reckless in a frenzy of making up for lost time, and they frequently get in trouble. Then their lives, and the lives of their wives and children, are hopelessly messed up. It can be lived through if his family has love for him, and he can consciously suppress his homosexuality—but he *knows*, and they *know*, and often, the devastating choice must be made by him to leave them if the conflicts engendered by his homosexuality are irreconcilable. True bisexuals may be able to handle a double life, but not easily.

Why would anyone want to go through the suffering that seems to be connected with "coming out"?

I have given you the impression that there is suffering, and there is. There is also a feeling—immense—of liberation in the admission to oneself of a predominately overt homosexual orientation, if, indeed, that is the truth. As to "wanting" to go through the process of coming out . . . how can I interpret for you the simultaneous inward experience (in the course of a person's coming out) of an irreversible drive, coupled with the choice of deciding to be what one is? For a homosexual human being, his time of coming out is a time of deciding to walk upright and consciously and proudly, along a course that he is bound to follow—and might otherwise traverse by being dragged along ignominiously.

You said that this period of "coming out" for a gay person can be particularly instructive for a straight person in terms of the development of a homosexual sensibility. How?

First, by keeping faith with the person who is coming out in human terms of kindness and consideration. If someone comes to you with an admission of homosexuality, it is no small matter to him, and he has trusted you with a profound secret. Second, "go" with him, if you can, while the reality of his unconscious needs begin and continue to assert themselves. Stay with him during this traumatic event; it will have violent ups and downs. Down, at first, perhaps, as he rebukes himself for what he may feel is a sin or sickness or a maladaptation of some kind. And then gradually up—as he reaches out, to you, to others, to the best in himself, and realizes that homosexuality is a part of him irrevocably, and that it is possible to live as a homosexual in the world, without shame or guilt. I would especially ask you to observe how that latter realization slowly takes root, and what a change it usually brings to every aspect of a young person who has come out. He walks taller, his voice becomes firmer, his skin (if it has erupted) clears up. He seems to have emerged from the dark night of his soul which had obscured every horizon for him—if indeed it did not render his whole life as a hoax and meaningless. As the conviction in him of his unconscious reality (in general—and in particular, his homosexuality) grows stronger, and with that strength, a feeling of validity replaces his self-doubt, you will have in your hands the trembling beginnings of a true and differentiated personality.

You will be amazed, as I am often, at how fast the person who really has come out grabs hold. He is suddenly capable of decisions and activities that will shape his entire life, whereas before he made a botch of everything he tried because of unconscious resistance: lack of fulfillment of his real emotional and sexual needs. Gaining this touch with his homosexuality, he has also gained touch with the deepest unconscious areas of his mind, the matrix of all that is creative within him. The "shadow-side" of himself has been acknowledged; a part of himself that he considered his "not-self" has come to light and been revealed as not so bad, and necessary to him if he is to grasp what it is to be a whole human being.

The opportunity of helping a young person—or an older one—through the experience of recognizing, understanding, becoming compassionate toward and actualizing his homosexual drive is a chance for you to witness firsthand the process of psychological rebirth.

Of what benefit is it to witness this?

The realization in a male of his homosexuality is a time of particularly dramatic and revealing growth of the unconscious mind. Ever "in process" toward a mysterious and awesome goal ("individuation" or the "unitive life"), the unconscious is here exposed at a pivotal moment: In one sense the ego of the emerging homosexual dies; in another sense, it is reborn. To have stood close by while this happened is to give you, if nothing else, a clear impression of unseen forces at work in all of us.

Is that important?

The pervasive sense of meaninglessness in our time is, I believe, due to loss of touch with, lack of compassion for the needs of, that unconscious mind. If gay people are sometimes forbidding and unfathomable and therefore frightening to straight people, it is partly because of the strange energies that gay people seemed to have tapped and harnessed in themselves. These energies, and the renewal that occurs when such energies are consciously shaped, are nothing but the gay person's irrevocable connection with his unconscious. It is important for you, as a straight person, to have that connection also, and it can be achieved the same way gay people achieve it: through *recognition* in yourself of your homosexual potential. You may not ever act on that potential—or even discuss it—but if you can muster the honesty to admit (in the degree I have previously indicated) its existence, you have put yourself in the way of tapping those unconscious energies also.

You will find your sense of personal identity stronger, more distinct, and not easily shaken if you cause yourself to become one of the few who have honestly, if only to yourself, admitted a homosexual potential.

You will feel a sense of relationship to all men, and you will have a keen insight into motives for thought or activity that had hitherto eluded you. If you are in business, this insight can be a valuable commodity in terms of pure cash, since you will be capable of appealing in part to the homosexual population, enlarging daily, with your product or service.

I should think touch with *your unconscious* is important. The example of someone in the process of coming out may be the one chance you have of coming to terms with the "numen" and "tremendum" of that most fertile and usually neglected part of yourself.

Chapter 7

How I Became Gay

How did you become gay?

How did I become gay . . . ? I have been stopped in my writing for almost a week while I faced that question. This afternoon, here in Provincetown, I had my usual yogurt for lunch, and I went for a bicycle ride out to the beach. I thought about how I had become gay. It is autumn now, and the roads are deserted, and the woods that I passed are oddly silent. Surf-casters dot the beach. It has been a curious day, rain predicted, but the Cape is always an exception. The rain held off, and instead, the sky had torn gray cloud banks, and it's been warm. I worked up enough perspiration to go for a swim in the pool at the Boatslip Motor Inn across the street from where I'm staying. Afterward, I returned to my apartment, dressed in white pants and a blue cotton T-shirt, and returned to the deck of the motel, where I ordered my afternoon vodka martini. Holding it, sitting in a canvas-back captain's chair facing the sea, I wondered about how I'd become gay.

Dare I say it: I have always been gay. Oh, I don't mean that there weren't crushes on little girls whose names I remember: Martha, Vera, Joan, and others, when I was in public school. But there were as many boys on that list of very young crushes, perhaps double the number. In fact, in those days, during the Great Depression, attending school in the West

93

Bronx, I was always in love. I can recall not being amused at all if I'd spent a day without having a crush on someone. In every new grouping of children, I'd seek out the one face, the one person, that appealed to me, and I'd yearn. Sometimes, I would get to know the person I liked, and then it was wonderful to spend an afternoon with him or her. If it happened to be a girl, the aunt and uncle with whom I lived would cluck kiddingly. They didn't seem to approve of my close friendship with boys, and once they overheard me calling a chum "dear" and "darling" and said to stop. Another time, they passed a vacant lot where I was wrestling with a clear-skinned boy of my dreams. I saw my aunt and uncle walk by, but they said nothing, and they did not look back. From the ages of nine to thirteen (1935 to 1939) I lived with them in a one-and-a-half-room apartment, after my mother died. Yes, I am fifty-one years old, though I don't feel it, and I sit in the afternoon on the deck of the Boatslip sipping a very dry martini.

Even before my mother died, there had been incidents of the kind that most boys experience: jokes about erections, jokes about girls; I can remember that I disliked all that intensely and I learned the word "vulgar" and used it often, and tried to stay aloof from those considerations which pressed upon my schoolmates, and I fell in love daily, and I masturbated continually, somehow, against a pillow propped under one leg, sans ejaculation.

The year before my mother died, she and I found refuge with her sister's family in Bedford, New York. I had two cousins, one slightly older, one slightly younger, than myself. The older one seemed to have been born as my nemesis. He teased and bullied me, and his brother performed as his mild-mannered accomplice. They threw my schoolbooks in the snow, they spat on me, they accused me of anything they could think of, which my aunt believed and my mother did not. My mother lay dying of cancer and a broken back and, I know now, a broken heart; my father had disappeared, my older brother had joined the Merchant Marine, and she and I were mendicants in the home of her sister. Yes, yes, my childhood sounds like bad Dickens, and I have been accused of exaggerating, but it was like that. I won't dwell on it. Strangely, in spite of everything, I remained a quietly joyous child, and how much I enjoyed the brilliant fall foliage laid on in the Bedford hills. In those hills, one autumn afternoon, as I crossed them with a friend on our way home from a one-room school, he told me to sit down, and he unbuttoned my fly and fondled my genitals, and I was not displeased.

My mother died; my life dissolved, but my body existed.

It was decided that I would be parceled out to another of my mother's sisters, who, as I mentioned, lived with her husband in a one-room apartment in the Highbridge section of the West Bronx. Before my mother died, I had lived in the Bronx with my own family, so I was able to return to the same public grade school I'd transferred from when Mother and I went to live in Bedford.

One and a half rooms! I slept on a cot in the kitchen. My aunt was kind and fun; my uncle sympathetic, but disinterested.

They had a neighbor with a key to the apartment, presumably so that when my uncle took my aunt to choir practice in New Jersey, on Thursday nights (for which she received six dollars) the man could look in to see if I was all right. When I was in bed on the cot, he would enter, pretend to bustle around, and then come to the cot and want to rub my tummy, as he put it, and he attempted to excite me and guided my unwilling hand to his pants. I despised him and I dreaded Thursday nights. But I felt sorry for him and recognized, I guess, that we had something terrible in common and I never told on him.

My father and brother dramatically reappeared on the scene. They were living in a three-room four-flight walk-up on Manhattan's West Side. The day of my public school graduation I went to live with them. I did not regret leaving the Bronx, and I rarely saw that aunt and uncle again, though I missed *her*. Years later, as I worked my way through Colgate University, she sent me an imitation fur coat which I was grateful for, and a few dollars in a letter now and then. My name for her was Dee, and I did miss her.

I enrolled at the High School of Commerce, which stood on West 66th Street where Lincoln Center is now. In my second year there, a wise teacher-counselor steered me off a career in banking, into classes that prepared me for an academic degree and, I hoped, college.

I lived with my father and brother in their verminous apartment, and I had a job lugging plates around town for a photoengraving company. I went to school from 9:00 to 1:30 and then to work as a messenger from 2:00 until 8:00 or 8:30, for $11.26 a week, plus the carfare I pocketed when I walked the delivery rather than take a bus. I supported myself, except when my brother gave me a quarter or my father prepared a dinner for me and his young paramour, a girl named Phyllis only ten years older than I. I despised her. (I don't anymore; nor do I blame my father.) Pop adored Phyllis, played the horses, and worked for the city as a dietician at the Mills Hotel, a flophouse for vagrants, where I went for dinner on Sunday after church.

At "Commerce" I had come to know and care for a Greek boy. We belonged to the same high school club, the Commerce Club, which was composed, would you believe, of supposedly the best elements of the student body. It pretended to exclusivity and the president had a little black notebook which had been handed down from club president to president from the early 1900s when the school was built and the club organized. The black book had in it an evaluation of all the members past and present. I adored my Greek friend and he seemed to like me and he taught me foil-fencing in the backyard of his family's little house on the far West side, and I came to know Greek people, and Greek food, and Greek ways, and my nascent homosexuality. He and I walked holding hands sometimes, or sat in movies with our arms around each other's seats (or holding hands), and I touted him as a candidate for president of the club and he was elected, and I was ecstatic and we went for long walks in Central Park on weekends and we fenced.

Our intimacy did not go unobserved; jealous club members took action. I was reviled, accused of terrible things, and he expelled me from the club by writing terrible things about me in the black book and removing my pin in a formal ceremony which I did not dodge—but worst, he expelled me from his heart, and then I was truly an outcast. At this time, I consciously realized my gay inclinations.

At home, affairs had worsened, my brother had married and was lost to me in densest suburbia and my father disliked having me around, and he hit me hard several times and I realized, at fifteen, that I must make it alone—away from Pop. I sold my treasured one-speed, balloon-tired red bicycle, got a room, transferred from day high school to George Washington *Night* High School, and got a full-time job as a mail boy for a company on East Forty-second Street. My life, incidentally, exemplifies *all* the theories as to how homosexuality originates.

My full-time day job and my night high school schedule began in the fall of 1942. Up at 7:30, to work by 9:00, through work at 5:00, home to a thirty-five-cent lunch-counter dinner and to grab my books, to night school at 7:00, finished there at 11:00, and home to do homework till 1:00 A.M. By fall, I was exhausted and frantic. I seemed to have no future. But I had one ace in the hole. I usually do.

Two events, one great and one small, were significant to me in 1942. Of course, Pearl Harbor had occurred the previous year, and I remember the sudden radio broadcast detailing it. I was aware by '42 that the stultified atmosphere of New York in the "depressed" thirties had dispelled, and that although it had taken a world war to do it, people seemed active again, more hopeful, and bound about important affairs. I had a vague idea that I would be called into service, but my first order of business was a college career: I was sixteen, and alone.

The second event of significance to me in '42 was my meeting with a boy in night high school who did not attract me—he fascinated me. I can't remember his name, so I shall call him Jimmy. Jimmy was an obvious homosexual, the queeniest kind: bleached blond hair, willowy, polished nails, and what I considered outlandish clothes, tight and bright. People who attended night school in those days were dedicated and exhausted, and they did not much have the time or energy to be friendly. The students in class were even less friendly to Jimmy. He was not attractive, and my interest in him was contrary to my ideas of beauty, but he drew me: I wanted to know how he managed to survive with so much seemingly going against him, how he could keep his sense of bitchy humor, of which I was aware he had an abundant supply, and how he presumed to live openly as a homosexual.

I remember one fall night *walking* with Jimmy the whole way down through Manhattan, as tired as I was and as tired as he must have been, from George Washington Night High School on 192nd Street to my room in an old building on Central Park West and Eighty-eighth Street: walking with Jimmy engaged in what was for me an astounding conversation. Jimmy lived for sex, and he brimmed over with his deeds and feats in the sexual arena, and he cruised constantly and supported himself by going to bed with old men he picked up on Forty-second Street. He was obviously interested in encouraging me to recognize my own homosexuality. I told him about my unconsummated "affair" with the Greek boy and he laughed at my naïveté. He flounced along beside me, and I recoiled with embarrassment from the looks of passersby, but we continued to walk and talk, and I could not leave him. I told him of my hope to go to college, and he offered to show me the ropes on Forty-second Street so that I could have money. But I knew I could not do it that way. For me, homosexuality was then what it has ever continued to be—a matter of aesthetic satisfaction, a thing that did not seem to count much for Jimmy.

Enroute as we walked, I asked Jimmy the same sort of questions that the questioner of this book has posed for the answerer, except that I wanted to know how to become gay—but, I decided despairingly, not in Jimmy's mode. I could not and would not believe that homosexuality had always to be so . . . vulgar. Still, I liked Jimmy at the end of that evening, and subsequently at school, for his defiant and even gallant spirit. He remained undaunted, and despised, and self-despising doubtless, but he survived, and in my opinion had carved out a life for himself based on a fuller realization of his human needs than I. It is right that the Jimmys of that long ago world are now considered among the true heroes of gay lib.

Oh yes, my ace in the hole . . . Rev. Dr. M., Princetonian, of great personal wealth, who happened to be the rector of R. Episcopal Church.

R. Episcopal Church and the parish house fronted on a small elegant park in lower Manhattan. I had attended it for all of my sixteen years, with curious regularity. It was a relief, after my week at work and night school, to meet the pleasant people there, and previous to that, the church had been my goal on Sundays, no matter where I was living, since I had been old enough to travel downtown on the el alone.

You see, my grandmother on my mother's side had begun attendance there in 1884 as a young married woman from Scotland when she and her husband and children lived on the Lower East Side. She had introduced young Rev. Dr. M., or just M. (his first name), by which he preferred to be known, to his parishioners on the day he had become rector. Although she and her family (my mother, etc.) had moved to Highbridge in the West Bronx (considered airy and clean: the Peter Cooper Village of its time), she and my mother and my mother's sisters all continued, more or less, to go downtown to R. Church, and considered it their own.

M. had conducted the funeral services for my grandmother, his old friend, and my mother, whose suffering he had known firsthand as he had come to see her often, especially in Bedford in her last days, where he, too, happened to have a house.

M. knew me well, as a baby and as a child (he had baptized and confirmed me), and now as a tired adolescent. I had never really had a talk with him, though he had often asked after my family, and he had expressed concern for me in my then difficult struggle to get by; he knew the circumstances of how I had left my father. I think I was shy of him, he seemed grand to me, and intellectual beyond my perceiving, although he had made me laugh during his sermons, which were often deliberately though subtly funny, and I seemed to appreciate his humor more than most of the parishioners. It had become a matter of course for him to say to me (and to me obscurely comforting) that if ever I had a problem that I couldn't cope with, to go to him and see if God and he couldn't handle it.

By the late fall of 1942, with night high school graduation imminent in the very early spring (war had altered the usual school schedules: one went to high school and college with three terms to the season and no long vacation), I had such a problem. *College*, which I wanted more than anything. And no way to go, in terms of money for tuition, not to mention expenses like clothes and suitcases and travel. Not one dime. I lived then with food and rent and carfare money for one week in advance, if I was lucky. Once in a while, my brother or my aunt in the Bronx or my father, whom I did not see much of, sent me two dollars in an envelope.

I went to M. and told him my problem. And now the story, mine, sad but honest so far, becomes real. M. put his arms around me and told me I would go to college somehow, and I did, that May of '43. I began as a freshman at Colgate University, proud of it as I had been proud of little else in my life up until then. I had a chance, it seemed to me, to be somebody—in fact, a writer, which I had decided early I wanted to be.

Although I had been to bed with no one before M., I can't say I went to him unknowing, nor can I say that as a lover, I felt a deep sexual attraction to him. I did not. But I loved him.

During that winter and spring before college, I was privileged to spend much time in his company, even to travel with him. He taught me the power in our lives of the unknown called God, and to be open and receptive always to what I received as guidance in prayer, and he gave me a glimpse in the person of himself, of what a civilized human being could be: a thing I had never seen close up. I was enthralled, and I was inspirited, and I was motivated to conceive of myself and hope to become just like him.

M. had a key to his personality; something that I have since learned that the Greeks had a word for—*arete*—which he had developed in his time at Princeton, along with F. Scott Fitzgerald and Edmund Wilson, and others who had gone to Princeton when he did and who had illuminated the era literarily. (I have since visited Princeton, the town and the university, for prolonged stays, and *arete* is the element in the air, which makes the place so free, so clear, so lovely.) I learned, or tried to learn, from M., this concept of *arete:* It is a kind of nobility of spirit, which shows itself as the driving force of a man's skill, power, and character—and it is especially a faithfulness in personal relations, a kind of honor that infuses those relations, above all. For me, it has devolved into a philosophy—no, that sounds too abstract—a principle of *decency,* to others and to oneself, that is *possible* to live up to. I suspect Greek boys got the same thing from association with their older male lovers, from whence the concept derives. Did I mention that a sense of humor helps implement that principle, and that M. encouraged that humor in me? It does, and he did.

As modest an accomplishment as it was, when I became editor of the Colgate humor magazine in my sophomore year, M. was particularly pleased. I had, by that time, put myself in the way of money from the G. I. Bill of Rights (I served in the Navy), and money from Colgate scholarships and jobs which I held, one at the library, the other at the Colgate Student Union where I dished up potatoes at 5 A.M. to the Naval contingent studying there. But M. never failed to come through when there was some insurmountable expense, and he told me that the parish house was my home when I was down from school. I saw him last in the early sixties, just before his death from cancer, and he told me as we embraced that I had become indeed "bone of his bone," and I considered his remark a high compliment indeed.

Did M. cause me to become gay? I think not. He caused me to hope that I might be homosexual and remain a man, and a real person, and that, as a writer, I had work in the world that I could and would accomplish. I repeat, I have always been gay.

Just before I left for Colgate, three weeks before, as a matter of fact, while I was still working and finishing up exams at night school, a curious incident occurred that also had definite bearing on how I became gay.

I allowed myself a walk on Sundays in the park along the Hudson River. It was a breezy spring afternoon, bright and filled with hope and excitement for me as I contemplated the wonderful experience at college that I was about to begin. Someone called to me, I turned, and it was a boy I had known casually (and admired from a distance) from my old poetry class at Commerce.

I shall call him Carl. He seemed delighted to see me, as I was him, and he wanted to know what had happened to me. Since he was blond and slim, and also sixteen, I told him everything, except about sex with M. He responded by inviting me to dinner. He lived with his family in a commodious and handsome apartment on the Drive. I had no idea that anyone who went to Commerce could have come from such a well-off background. Actually, his family was restless, and he'd moved around a lot with them, and Commerce for him had been only an interlude between his sessions in prep schools; he himself was scheduled to begin at Princeton, as I was at Colgate, that summer.

His mother was a tall and gracious woman, his father a hail-fellow-well-met sales executive, and they had as a permanent guest in the apartment a whiskey-voiced woman who served simply as a friend.

Carl's family drank a good deal, which made the atmosphere excessively convivial, and we sang songs that spring afternoon and evening around the piano—old sentimental musical comedy love songs that I liked, and still like, and that I used to sing with the Greek boy, after the formal part was over at the Commerce Club meetings. With Carl and his family, we sang "Golden Days" from *The Student Prince* at least ten times.

The upshot was that since my life was at so crucial a juncture, and since I lived in a room alone, I should come and stay with them in that huge, sun-flooded apartment overlooking the Drive and the river and the tall cliff-banks on the Jersey shore, until the morning I took the train from Grand Central on my way to college. I did so, Carl helped me move—and I had a sense of life opening up into high drama and great expectations indeed. No "poor-boy" Dickens character ever felt more hope in his heart.

I sat on a couch with Carl, the second night of my arrival, quite late, and his family was out, and we had put on some sentimental phonograph records, and the moon glittered on the Hudson, and we kissed, and we went to bed and made love—for me, the first experience in which I had participated heart and soul. At the end of those incredible two weeks with Carl, and in close touch with M. also, I knew that my course as a homosexual was set irreversibly, that I had found what I required sexually and spiritually. Did Carl make me gay? No, as I said, I have always been gay. Carl taught me ecstasy —golden days, sunshine of our merry youth, days of innocence and truth . . . life has nothing sweeter than its springtime, golden days . . . when we're young, golden days. . . .

This day's sunlight of my merry middle age is fading on the deck of the Boatslip, my cocktail glass is empty, and now, if I hurry, I have just time for dinner before the seven o'clock news.

Chapter 8

Fears That Beset

What is the fuss about having members of the National Gay Task Force monitor in advance programs that portray a homosexual character? What do homosexuals fear?

Gay people are justified in their fear of grimly biased dramatic presentations of themselves and various aspects of gay life. Such portrayals simply perpetuate the stereotypes that caused trouble in the first place, such as showing a gay person to be "mincing" or "limp-wristed" or notably "catty" or "bitchy" or so susceptible to blackmail as to reveal important "secrets" rather than be exposed personally, or themselves as blackmailers of straight people who "lapsed" in the past. A "type" is established dramatically by incessant portrayal of homosexuals possessing those characteristics. It is unfair, unjustified by the behavior of the majority of homosexuals who are decent people. It is a cheap way for a writer to sketch in a "bad" guy. That must be stopped, and stopped cold if gay people are to attain to the individuality and dignity they seek and deserve. Such portrayals are fearful things, and wrong.

But aren't those characteristics sometimes true of homosexuals?

Stereotypically *only*. I've known ad executives with the proverbial five kids who are as swishy and bitchy and evil in their human relationships as the worst queen in the cheapest Eighth Avenue dive bar. The stereotypical homosexual as the bad guy is on a par with the shuffling black servant, the Indian as a wild man, the Jew as a shylock, the German as a Nazi, and the Englishman as effete. Cliches! These cliches perpetuate the awful attitude some straight people maintain toward gay people, which is implemented in life by various discriminatory procedures and outright violence—no wonder, if viewers' minds are filled with such rot. It is being stopped by the gay organizations monitoring such programs in advance and insisting that gay people are not made scapegoats.

What are some of the other fears peculiar to the homosexual?

At this late date, homosexuals still fear exposure at their jobs. It is the rare employer who genuinely understands gay people as gay people. The employer who says, "I don't care what people do off their jobs as long as they do their work on their jobs," is ducking the issue. The day may come when a homosexual incident occurs on the job, as heterosexual incidents occur on the job, or the day may come when a gay person feels bereft of his lover, and performs poorly at his job, just as a heterosexual employee suffering through divorce proceedings may perform poorly or not at all at his job. That is the test of a liberal employer, whether or not he can take the gay employee as a whole man, drawbacks with pluses, on the job *and* personally—as an employer must take a heterosexual, does take the heterosexual employee as a matter of course. Gay people are rightfully afraid on their jobs of accusers of narrow mentality who may shake the confidence of a quasi-liberal boss, regardless of how well that gay person does his job. Although most gay people learn to live with this, it demands constant dissembling, and, fear of exposure—or of being harassed to distraction by "kidders" at work—is real.

Are there other job-connected fears?

There is one other fear on the part of gay people in business which, however, is somewhat less tangible than the fears I've mentioned.

What is it?

I have observed that sharp, straight business people dealing with acknowledged gay people offering an individual talent in some special area often deal with them summarily or bluntly cheat them. There is a pervasive conviction among those sharp, straight business people that somehow a gay person will not resort to law to gain his agreed-upon due. That gay people lack the clout personally or through their representatives to enforce agreements. That gay people or their representatives would be embarrassed by public attention focused upon them if homosexuality were even a peripheral issue of the affair in contention. I think many gay people have had this experience with commercial interests, where an a priori assumption exists that gay people can be gypped with impunity. It is something I as a gay person fear, because, often, sharp business people believe it and then a situation develops that cannot be subverted in advance.

Since "looks" seem to be so important in gay life, do most homosexuals fear growing old?

Yes, to some degree, I think this is a fear that besets gay people unwarrantably. It is a fear of people who are mostly not yet old. They fall into the conviction that no one will love them when they are old because "looks" mean so much to them at the moment, and they believe their major appeal to others is on the basis of their "looks." As they grow older, in fact, "looks" may still be important to them as a quality of people they desire, but they begin to find, happily (if they've done something with their lives), that "looks" aren't as important to *others* as they had thought. That others are attracted to them for different reasons: new reasons, valid reasons. They discover that "experience" in the world at large is a highly attractive attribute to others, that it "turns on" prospective bedmates as "looks" rarely did in the early days. And, yes, this fear of losing their "looks" does lead gay people to a greater-than-average preoccupation with health and exercise. It can lead to depression for a mature homosexual in his lonely or nostalgic hours. But I don't think for long.

Are homosexuals afraid of commitment to one lover?

Wary is a better word; these days, "uncommitted" relationships seem to be the rule. Not many pairs of lovers have made definite down-to-the-ground vows to one another. Tacit agreements seem more acceptable, and those tacit agreements allow for lapses. I wonder if this hasn't come about because gay people in hitching up with a lover did so too quickly in years past, and made bad bargains, and let themselves in for a lot of suffering. Collective gay experience now indicates some caution, which I think in the long run is wise. But then, isn't it always the extraordinary individuals who will "sign up" body and soul to someone they love? They don't hardly make 'em like that anymore, as the saying goes, homosexual or heterosexual. I am inclined, on the basis of relatively short acquaintance, to take a chance, to fall in love, to make a commitment, and I have paid a high price emotionally for my mistakes. But I can tell you now, I wouldn't have done it any other way. The intense joy of knowing that someone loved me without reserve, and that I loved him without reserve, is a feeling I would not have missed.

But the "look" of gay life today, is "uncommitted." You can see it in the disco dancing. As an elderly woman friend of mine commented, "Why they never touch!" . . . they bob and weave and gyrate, but indeed, they hardly ever touch . . . no role of leader or follower is discernible, which is, *out of bed*, a good way to have it . . . they jump and squirm and undulate, but they hardly ever touch.

Sitting at the disco bar of the Boatslip (in the summer there is a dance session at tea time, which I like), it dawned on me that perhaps the dancers of the modern era touched in a way that the close dancers of the past did not. Disco dancers do dance together in their fashion: Their movements, if you watch closely, are synchronized by body signals, and other non-verbal methods of communication—with the "beat" regulating the tempo between them. That kind of psychological touching is certainly characteristic of the young these days, and perhaps it is more efficacious than meets the eye, regarding initiating a sexual contact.

Who would know about it as authoritatively as my friend Reggie Cabral, who owns the famous Atlantic House bar and disco here in Provincetown; I stopped by and asked him: "Do they get together, Reggie, as often and as happily after disco dancing as people used to after close dancing?"

"Better," Reggie said, laconically.

My friend Peter Ryder, who owns the Boatslip, concurred, as did Jack Rubin, manager of the multi-dance-floored Town House. These places, by the way, are gay landmarks, and the decency and concern of the proprietors for their gay clientele is exemplary. You would enjoy an evening in all three places.

So—it may be that the not touching of disco dancers suits, in that it does reflect the nature of gay "uncommitted" relationships: deafeningly frank, wildly sensual—not intimate in the old-fashioned sentimental way, but with a subtle regard for the exigencies of human relationships after all.

Do gay people ever fear one another?

Sometimes gay people try to frighten one another. If two of them are interested in the conquest of the same "trick," they're capable of "menacing" that is offensive as well as offending. At its worst, the two contending suitors go for the *financial* jugular. In an attempt to persuade a boy to hitch his wagon to *his star*, each offers the boy what amounts to a statement of fiscal status, and a denunciation of the other party as insolvent, in debt, and insane. You would think that such heavy ammunition might be resorted to only in extremity; it isn't. A casual pick-up in a bar can occasion a passionate "worth" fight between two otherwise calm and respectable and responsible gay people. The old clichés, "I'll ruin you," or "I can buy and sell you," or "He hasn't a pot to piss in," are the most often exchanged rejoinders. At this point, in a bar, the boy in contention begins to feel like an article in an auction, and like as not, goes off with some third party who's been sitting quietly in a corner watching the fracas and waiting for a chance to catch the boy's eye. Financial undercutting is an old and tired ploy, nor is it an unknown device among heterosexuals. An obnoxious variation of this theme is when money is used by a rich homosexual to plunder for his evening's pleasure—he promises to "take care" of someone he's just met, when he has no intention of the kind. A younger gay would have reason to fear such a looter, to distrust him and to dismiss him. The whole dreary routine of "impressing" someone into going to bed is too obvious to work anymore: The kids are wise, and one's presumed gay friends are outraged by such crude tactics.

Do gay people fear impotence?

Not much. Impotence, I believe, is far less a concern to gay people than to straight people. Gay people have alternatives. (I am excluding impotence due to liquor, fatigue, etc., or due to some physical injury.) If a gay person finds that he is verging on impotence—few allow it to overcome them—with his long-term lover, he can vary his sexual routine with that lover, by adding a third individual to the usual twosome in bed. This can be done readily, and not much fuss made about it. Or, without breaking his lover relationship out of hand, the impotent lover can avail himself of a night at the baths to undo the tension of his mental/sexual logjam. Or find a partner in the street with whom he spends only a few minutes. Anonymous sex, brief, passionate. Those are possible gay ways to resuscitate a flagging libido.

Another method of subverting impotence with one's lover is to change roles; the dominant partner submits, the submissive partner dominates. Mostly, for lovers, this activity is unsatisfactory, and they return to the customary roles with relief and gusto, but the changeabout has performed its function.

How about premature ejaculation?

Delightful, not a handicap to fear, but a plus attribute. I have found that fast ejaculators are good for a second or even third time—and as we all know, it's better the second or third time around.

Do gay people fear mental problems?

Who wouldn't, forced to live a split-level existence such as gay people have had to live until recently. But the situation has changed drastically, especially for the young. I have lived long enough to have myself witnessed the change.

When I went to Colgate, queers were an abomination, the ultimate one. Anybody suspected of being queer was hounded for it. A crowd of upperclassmen once chased me through dormitory corridors because I had let my hair grow into a bang across my forehead and in their estimation my hair was an insult to their country and to their alma mater and to their malehood. (It was wartime, remember, and many breasts were pounded a la Tarzan to prove maleness.) I escaped the rampaging horde by taking refuge with an old mathematics teacher who lived in a room in the dorm as proctor. (The closest, really, that I've ever been to the subject of math; since wartime schedules pertained, and *serious*-subject classes like math and physics were jammed, I was able to concentrate my time exclusively on *un*serious courses in literature, philosophy, and psychology.) But the next day, under faculty advisement, I made sure that the bang was cut off.

That action became indicative. I began to think I must be plain *crazy* to be so different from the rest. The ideals and the charm I'd learned from M., and my one experience of sexual ecstasy with Carl, went out the window. Although I knew my homosexuality consciously, I held the opinion that everyone else held: I was essentially *balmy*, and I must watch my step so that no one found out and I would not be expelled from college. You can imagine that I lived in a state of terror.

I had little "traveling money" and rarely got away from Colgate even on holiday vacations. I spent my vacation reading "mere" literature in the old stone library—oh, the hot summer day I discovered Mann's *Death in Venice!* What horizons opened! Still, Ashenbach faired poorly in his love for Tadzio, and, as a homosexual at Colgate, I was dying my own death. But the story gave me heart—there had been somebody in the world who felt as I did. The work of Oscar Wilde I'd read, and thrilled to also, but the frank interpretations of his life and work had yet to be written. Then, even during those holidays when I had a little money to celebrate, I went to New York and stayed at the parish house—and M.'s attitude toward the sexual act was "do it and forget it." Though he taught me *arete*, he did not teach me how to deal with myself as a homosexual, and I began to see that the ideals of the thing did not take care of the trouble one could get into, *in one's own mind*.

Clearly, the judgment of society branded homosexuality as *abnormal*, and during those war years, abnormality and its uselessness to the war effort (its presumed inefficiency primarily) qualified homosexuals for mental institutions. So I hitched my sanity to my capacity to reason, which was held in high esteem then (the faculty for coolly maneuvering a PT boat abaft the torpedo of a marauding German submarine). I became very reasonable; I tried to reason away my homosexuality. Because I have a strong will, I almost reasoned my sexual needs out of existence, at least any outward show of them, and I was able to continue. I would pay the price in the future with anxiety attacks of severe and long duration, requiring analysis, but I remained in college.

Contrast my situation then, if you will, to the situation of kids who are gay in college now. Not only is it "in" to be gay or bisexual, it is to hold some (admired) secret of a full life. Classes or seminars or simply isolated speeches on any aspect of homosexuality can depend upon a standing-room audience. Books and pamphlets on the subject are readily available and dispensed with alacrity from college libraries where whole sections are devoted to the subject-category! (Try to find a thing about homosexuality in my old college library; one looked timidly in large dictionaries merely to find the word "homosexual.")

Today, on campuses there are gay student organizations. If someone does not understand his homosexuality, or any part of it, he can go and have it explained to him in detail, immediately, and sometimes be personally instructed!

There are the gay college dances: bright, handsome affairs, filled with delight and charm. Three years ago, I went to Rutgers University, for the gay dance there, held in the Postgraduate Hall on campus and I expected from my experience at Colgate that the red-necked hordes would be waiting outside with shotguns. Waiting outside! Ha! What looked to me like most of the red-neck football and basketball players were *inside*, bearded and wearing dresses, dancing their fool heads off with boys they would have clobbered on sight thirty years ago. Laughter and good feeling at Rutgers. No one waited outside: no one, that is, except the disapproving ghosts of the past, dishonored specters still proclaiming the madness of it, but slinking away into the night, and taking with them their accusations of insanity for being homosexual.

Yes, gay people still have mental problems, as everyone has, but less so than in the past. It is when they must come in contact with the world of their fathers, who were raised as I was on a diet of hate for "abnormality," the world in which they must earn a paycheck, that the mental problems of living as a homosexual, overtly or covertly, begin. And some gay people feel these problems severely enough to need psychological assistance, and the adjustment to an overt or covert gay life is rough. But I believe that their liberal early experience as gay people, plus the fact of support of their homosexuality as *not insane* from so many effectively functioning gay organizations, keeps them from the depths of despair that used to be the rule for "queers." And as young adults, the fear of being institutionalized for their differentness is almost nonexistent. Amen!

Are black homosexuals subject to special fears that beset?

Not special ones. As a minority, maybe double the portion. But as you know, black is beautiful, and black *and* gay is *gorgeous*. They'll survive.

So—fears that beset. Another step in our exploration of what it is like to be gay. The right to openly possess your emerging homosexual sensibility was hard-won, and is still being fought for. But the element of fear in gay people has lessened.

Chapter 9

Family Relations

What advice can be given to a mother and father who have just found out about a gay son?

Although we have touched on this in Chapter 6, I do want to answer your question in more specific detail.

There are three things to do right away.

1. In a confrontation with your gay offspring, stop and listen to what he has to say, and allow him time for pauses and digressions.

2. As he talks about himself, resist firmly your inclination to assign "blame" either to him or to yourself. (A) He has not by his orientation deliberately tried to thwart your hopes for his future. Although the lack of grandchildren may seem at this point a confirmed fact, and the question of whether or not to give him his inheritance may arise in your mind—hold off ill-considered expression of disappointment, or suspicion of his impaired sense of responsibility. (B) No, you didn't go wrong someplace in raising him.

3. Accept his offer (and if he is wise, he will make it) to read up on the subject of homosexuality, and even to meet his gay friends, before you call in your priest or minister or rabbi or psychoanalyst—or your neighbors next door who had a similar problem and who solved it by kicking out their misguided "monster."

But why should I hold off with my natural reaction?

Because the situation you are dealing with is a frequent one nowadays. It has been lived through and successfully resolved by your predecessors, and it has always been your rule to learn from experience. I simply want to save you from making the worst mistakes at the outset, when the worst mistakes occur. Your thoughtless words spoken to a gay offspring who has just revealed himself are the words that are longest remembered by him and by you, such as "obscene," "weird," "pansy," and the mutual forgiveness needed from you both may be years in forthcoming.

This situation is so familiar by now that Laura Z. Hobson, with a canny mind for exploring the large issues of the day, has codified it step by step in her book *Consenting Adults*. If your son doesn't urge you to read it, I do, with a proviso. Ms. Hobson will show you, in the person of the main character, a mother who has "just found out and has to live with it," that you with your gay son are not alone. But Ms. Hobson prettifies the situation. Her son goes off with a professional man (into the sunset) at the end, to live a life of dignity and devotion. Your son, on the other hand, may just have come across the delights of whoring, and his adjustment to homosexuality may be unpalatable to you. Bear with, oh, bear with him, as he drinks to the dregs this new cup of pleasure that has been put into his hands. He will calm down, and get himself together when the glitter-dust of his self-discovery begins to settle. These days of his self-discovery are usually a happy time for him; its most perilous aspect, his need to deal with you.

Suppose I do hold off from an out-and-out scene, but I call someone for help?

That's fine, and again, if your son is wise, he will look into what help you offer. It may be, indeed, that his homosexuality is an experiment (kids these days experiment with everything) or he's imitating some admired schoolmate or some androgynous rock star whose music he plays to your distraction; that for him, a homosexual episode is just a one-shot thing. In that case, good counseling can get him and get you over the

114

rough spot, patience and time will avail, and he will find his heterosexuality again.

It might be wise to consult a *gay* counseling service. You must *not* distrust such a service to secretly induce your son to be gay because its members are gay. No one can make your son gay if he is truly heterosexual. They will simply present him with the facts and truths of what a gay life is like, and with their help he may begin to see that he was only passing through a phase and that living and loving as a homosexual is not for him. His heterosexual drives will assert themselves, never fear, and if he has had a gay experience and realizes it is not for him, he will be a stronger and wiser heterosexual. He will know from his experience what homosexuality is about, that there's nothing to be afraid of, nor be intriguingly mystified by—that it doesn't satisfy him, period.

If, on the other hand, you son *is* gay (though not exclusively), then a gay counselor can, again, get you and him over the rough spots—help you adjust to the facts, and help him to adjust to himself and to you. I mean if you deny him his reality, the counselor can be of help to him. If you accept it, you will need support as the ramifications of his gay life become apparent. Alas, as per Ms. Hobson's book, not all middle-class gay sons pick as their lovers neat and respectable professional men. Sometimes they pick a rough or raunchy character: garage mechanics, truck drivers, or ditsy queens head the list. You'll be amazed how nice they can be on their best behavior.

Suppose he doesn't tell me?

And you suspect. Well, chances are you have indicated you don't want to know. That is a valid method of procedure. As a matter of fact, I would mostly advise young people *not* to put themselves or their parents through such a hassle if they can possibly contain their "secret."

Do they take your advice?

Some see the wisdom of it but tell their parents anyway. It seems to be a compulsion that is irresistible for a gay boy to tell, at least his mother. He hopes that the pal-like relationship with her that he has always enjoyed will deepen if she knows him as he really is. I advise such gay people that they may be right, but there is a better chance that his admission will drive a stake through the heart of that friendship. For a parent to understand that her boy is gay is to have to recognize that he has grown up, that he has a range of sexual/emotional needs exclusively his own, which a parent cannot fulfill—and points to their separation—*unless* as a parent, you can grasp this superb opportunity to develop your own homosexual sensibility, and proceed with your son vicariously as he discovers the particular problems he faces, and as he fights through to a resolution of those problems. Your standing by with interest and love can hasten the process for him to a satisfactory conclusion—and you will know down to the ground what it is like to be gay.

Is there a significant generalization to be made about the reactions of brothers or sisters of a boy who's come out?

Yes. They're often the first to know. In fact, your son may have had some tight talks with a sister or brother of his before he ventured to tell you. And if the siblings are in roughly the same age group, the chances are they will react with greater understanding than you are able at first to muster. Further, it is not uncommon in a large family for him to have a brother or sister also on the same course. I have never known or heard of a brother or sister of a gay boy who outright rejected him. I have known many families where a gay boy was the most admired and respected member, and often the person to whom the others turned for sympathy and advice with *their* problems.

What will the neighbors think?

What they always think: the worst. You may have to put up with smiles from them that are inexplicable, especially if your son has tried to make their son, and failed. If, on the other hand, your son succeeded, then you and your neighbor have new common ground for gossip, as behooves mothers-in-law. I think what the neighbors think is a small price to pay for your son's psychological well-being. And then I could be wrong; if you tell your neighbor what your son has told you, the look of relief on your neighbor's face as she tells you about the clandestine activities of her husband may more than repay your trust and confidence in her. What coffee-break conversations you'll have!

Should I accept an invitation from my gay son to go to his apartment for dinner with him and his lover?

By gad, you'd better. The evening will probably be the world turned topsy-turvy for you, but you will see the world as gay people see it every day. No, you don't have to stand up whenever your son's lover enters the room; no, you shouldn't ask either of them when they're going to get married; no, you mustn't ask, "Where's the *other* bed?" (they both sleep, together, with one another, probably often in embrace, in that little narrow bed that serves as a couch in the living room and on which you're sitting). Yes, do bring a bottle of booze; yes, do extend an invitation to them to come together for dinner at your house; yes, you may *not* expect them to abandon words or gestures of affection when they are in your presence. If you let yourself, you'll have a grand time; newlywed gay boys usually eat and serve great food (they need the strength for sex), and you will probably find their stereo music wistfully moody with plaintive songs by black women performers, and if you can bring yourself to get slightly or very high with them, the rightness of their relationship and the logic of it, which may have seemed strange to you, will suddenly come into focus. You will have to agree you have rarely seen your son so at one with himself, and so seemingly directioned about his life. If, during the course of the evening and as the drinks begin to wear off, you are back with your original opinion about the absurdity of the couple you're visiting, don't worry—after a few dinners and parties with both of them, your opinion when "high" will come to sustain itself. You may even learn to be proud of your son and his friend. Especially when their business together begins to pay off, and they offer you that vacation in Europe you've always wanted to take.

Even if my son adjusts to his new gay life, didn't I fail him in his upbringing?

Yes, take the responsibility on yourself—you were too over-protective or too uninterested in him in his early years. You never did see to his meals properly and that cook you used to have gave him hot dogs whenever he cried. As Mame asked in the musical, did he need a helping hand (you were off playing golf when he fell and broke his leg); did he need a stronger hand (you let him have his teddy bear till he was twelve); did you ever turn away (you hid the look of chagrin when he interrupted that elegant dinner party with a sex question); did you set a bad example (he never saw you without a martini). By all means *take the blame*. By the same token, if your son and his lover do build a lasting relationship between them, which eventuates in their radiant personal happiness, or in a business or artistic enterprise that means something in the world (as well as lots of money), you can *take the credit:* It was you, after all, who counseled your son always to have imagination, be willing to take a chance, hold out for the gold ring on the merry-go-round of life, to follow his own heart no matter how strait the gate and in spite of all opposition to his own self be true! It was you, really, who glimpsed, as only a parent can, his "differentness" at an early age, and you who had the daring to encourage it.

Either way, blame or credit, you have taken the possibility away from your offspring that he could have had any part in the decision or responsibility for his choice of sexual orientation. And you have implied that no one—your son—in his right mind would actually *want* to be gay.

But suppose my son falls in love with a person who is as old as, or older than, I. How can I face that?

Do what the families of Greek boys did in regard to their son's male suitor—see if he really suits. Look up his standing in the community, his business ability, his trust fund, his bank account. If he is someone who has succeeded in life, it may be that that will-o'-the-wisp bleached-blond son of yours can learn a few things. If, however, he's just some old guy whose line that beautiful son of yours has fallen for, call the police!

118

No, don't call the police, I'm kidding. But make a fuss; it is your right absolutely, as would be the case if your marriageable daughter were taken in by a flim flam man—reveal the bounder for what he is. If the old guy does an about-face, however, and proves he is heir to a company listed in Fortune's top five hundred, and travels about incognito so people won't seek him for his money, you do a faster about-face and welcome him into your family with love everlasting, resting secure in the knowledge that the dummkopf you spawned may have hit the jackpot after all: Visualize yourself on the fantail of a hundred-eighty-footer, being served black Russians by a white-coated steward: It'll ease your pain. Oh, the yacht is moored off the French Riviera, of course.

Won't my gay son abuse his financial inheritance?

You mean you're afraid he'll say "Drinks on me for everyone" four or five times a night. No, he'll go to Europe (if you leave him more than two beans), and he'll hole up in a small hotel in Taormina or Capri or Amsterdam, and he will love deeply and long when he is young, and when he is old, he'll return to America and dress for dinner, and read a lot, and give charming intimate dinner parties and talk gracefully to the young and gay at his table about the meaning of existence, the beauty, the ravishing beauty of it. And his gay lawyer friend will have tripled the capital you left him, and he will endow an orphan asylum with new linen and a comfortable game room and people will say of him when he's dead that he was a great old queen, and generous. I can think of worse things to happen to the inheritance you leave him.

What do I do if my gay son comes running home, having made a mess of things?

Give him refuge without question: his old room back, plenty of Kleenex, chicken soup (if that's an old family remedy), and your heart and your ear. Living as a gay person in the world is not easy, I can't say that too often. If he's bungled his job, assure him he can get another. If he's bungled his love relationship and his lover calls, take messages. If it is apparent to

119

you that love still exists between them, invite the lover over.

Twice you will be offered sharpest insight into what it's like to be gay: during the "coming out" process, and during the recoil process of unhappiness after a love affair. During those processes, all of the conundrums, conflicts, and sadnesses of being gay stand forward; there is no ducking problems. But in the background of this suffering, you will sense the larger picture of two people having loved, having been happy together, and having been creative in one another's lives, as well as destructive. You will sense that the grieving figure before you was infinitely involved; that he participated in the most magnificent experience a human being can have: He was loved and he loved in return. So what if his life has caved in now. You know and must tell him that he has gained ground and that if indeed his present love relationship is over, he will love again more wisely. Time is what is required here, time for reflection—so let him mope, and brood if he chooses, and bear with him while he spills details you may not understand or want to hear, and give him simple tasks to do to divert him momentarily. It is a taxing thing, seeing a person through a breakup, but if you can do it, you will be of utmost help in the ways I've mentioned and your homosexual sensibility will be significantly deepened.

What becomes of the relationship between parents and a gay son?

If at first you as parent took the news according to the old scenario of how can you do this to me, you beast, monster, etc., and you threw the baggage out—of course the wounds will take longer to heal.

But I can tell you this: It is a hardhearted pair of parents who do not with the years come around to forgiveness, and understanding that there is nothing to forgive; that their son's homosexuality was inevitable and right for him. If you as a parent are bound to religious tradition, to middle-class values and respectability, it may take a personal tragedy to bring you and a gay son or daughter back together in the same house. But that reunion will occur. Why postpone it until you are too stricken with grief to make an effort? It requires the merest gesture from you of lifting a telephone receiver: "Hello,

Bobby, this is Mother. Just wondering how you are. . . . Not too well since Dad died, but I'm trying. You okay? How's your friend? . . . Yes, I'd like to, or better, why don't you both come up here? . . . Yes, next Friday will be fine, stay the weekend. . . . I love you. . . ." As simple as that.

Chapter 10

Fidelity and Infidelity

Why have "fidelity" and "infidelity" been hitched together?

Because I want those two concepts related in your mind. *The fact that gay love affairs are tough to sustain leads often to infidelity.* If gay people knew more about the emotional truths (the psychological mechanics of their love relationships), they might be better at keeping the lover they already have, and better able to resist a temptation to infidelity.

Is the lack of societal sanction a real reason for the shaky ground of gay relationships, promoting easy infidelity and breakups?

I wish it were. The answer to your question is a flat no. Lovers aren't unfaithful to one another because they can't write their names as "married" in the town ledger, nor because a wedding ceremony is not performed in church, nor because they can't file joint income tax returns. To legitimatize gay relationships would be fine, and lessen fear for gay people, and I *do* agree with that statement by gay-libber Barbara Gittings, that the goal of the political gay lib movement is to have gay relationships considered on a par with straight relationships. But that is not going to have a major effect on the reasons why gay people in love can't "keep it together." As you know, societal sanctions aren't doing much to guarantee longevity for heterosexual relationships.

What are the "psychological mechanics" of love relationships that gay people ought to know that would help keep them faithful?

To review, they must know about role-playing.

What is it that they must know about role-playing, the major thing?

To review further: the major thing about role-playing is to settle on and maintain their more-than-not sexual stances in bed (and out of bed if that has been mutually agreed upon).

Why is it so difficult for a gay lover to settle on his more-than-not role?

Because it calls for an exercise in introspection, and total honesty with himself in terms of examining his past to ascertain what role he has mostly played across the years, and enjoyed mostly. And then, having accomplished that wisdom, he must henceforward play his role efficiently and assume the *responsibility* it entails toward his partner, and also the responsibility for consciously suppressing most of the time any other role that might occur to him. If he is more-than-not dominant in a relationship, it behooves him to consciously suppress a minor need to be submissive on occasion, and vice versa for the submissive partner. (Conscious suppression, by the way, differs from unconscious repression in that it is an act of will and rarely harmful.)

124

But why must the obverse role be suppressed?

To preserve the necessary illusion in the mind of one's lover, of one's "primary" dominance or submissiveness, especially at the start of a relationship. Later on, when both lovers are confirmed in their more-than-not *true* roles beyond a shadow of a doubt in both minds, then and only then can they sometimes do a flip-flop in regard to their more-than-not major role, and not violate the major role-playing premises on which the relationship was founded.

Is it possible to be more graphic on this point?

I mean that the more-than-not dominant partner can roll over (submit) and allow himself to be anally penetrated once in a while by his more-than-not submissive lover, and the more-than-not submissive lover can lie back (dominate) once in a while and be fellated by his more-than-not dominant lover. *But* if "once in a while" turns into "most of the time," then one or both lovers are going to lose interest. The original premises of the relationship have been drastically changed. In fact, a complete reversal has taken place, and unless the lovers are extraordinary people or extraordinarily in love, the relationship collapses, essentially because of contradicted illusions and consequent lack of satisfaction in the bedroom. The time is ripe for infidelity on the part of one or both. In my mind, this is the major reason for breakups. Both partners have labile egos, subject to slippage and reversal, and unless that is recognized and a measure of control exerted, relationships become mishmash and subject to change, dissolve, without notice.

Is it to be inferred that fidelity might pertain if lovers made gay love more of an art?

Exactly. There is no such thing as a "lawyer" or a "doctor" or a "statesman" or a "clerk"—*people* train for and play the *roles* that they have assigned themselves (which they then permit others to expect of them). In a gay love relationship *that functions well:* Each lover plays his self-assigned, more-

125

than-not *true* role. If he doesn't, if he abandons that role midstream, then the relationship is emotionally adrift, and "abandon ship" via infidelity follows.

Is this known to two lovers in a relationship that functions well and for whom fidelity is no effort?

Most of the time not consciously; it just happens to them and they are happy together, pursuing clearly out of bed what is best for each, and in bed, compatible.

And for the unlucky ones?

The imperative psychological "union of opposites" does not occur, and they are unable to set up a reliable sexual modus vivendi between them. They are unable to establish and maintain *roles*.

Must a love affair and fidelity be the end-all and be-all for every gay individual?

No, I suppose not. I have heard a good case made for the validity of *not* having a love affair, which is different from merely being promiscuous. Still, it is my conviction that *in the foundation layers of the human psyche, there exists a need for that one person with whom to share the deepest and most significant experiences of life.* Although gay life may stud itself with sparkling innovations, that need pertains in most of us, and perhaps most severely in those who are most promiscuous—*they are still looking.* If they had not hope, their promiscuity would decrease and the energy diverted to other channels. They *do* still hope to find that one individual who can heal them, mend their dividedness, but their expectation of aid from another, from "outside," is unreal. It is *they* who must *heal themselves* within, *before a love relationship is possible.* A gay person can subsist on casual love and sex relationships, but it is meager fare, as opposed to the wonder and delight of a love transference that endures.

What is the self-healing process?

Self-examination: If the motor does not work, one looks under the hood. Dirty sometimes, but a must if the engine is to be fixed, the person made whole and fit for a lover. Dirty in that certain balky tendencies (destructive desires toward himself and toward others) come to light in the person who is constantly searching. Anyone he's involved with emotionally becomes the target of his unconscious hostility (a residue from whatever source in the past). If a gay person is in a perpetual state of inner torment, of emotional and spiritual disrepair, he is hardly able to exert any control over his compulsive nature, much less consciously impose upon it any required design for living or loving. I have observed that such people often function in their careers, but the moment love or even an emotional attachment begins to form, they panic and act their worst—and are therefore denied *what I feel makes my gay life worthwhile: the living presence of a lover*. But sometimes one can get by tolerably without a fulfillment that one has never known . . . or only known a little, a long time ago. For those who cannot get by, self-examination with or without an analyst is called for loudly.

Isn't "do your own thing" and consequent infidelity a prevalent idea among the young and gay?

Yes, among the *very* young and gay—until they want to accomplish something in life which is a bit more demanding than smoking pot or disco dancing, both of which are admirable, you understand, but not as full-time occupations. I had a lover years ago who insisted upon doing his own thing, in which direction he was influenced by his young friends, to the detriment of our relationship, among other detriments. Today he stands in impressive connection with humankind, and *not* doing his own thing, but doing *God's thing*—he is an important member of the entourage of a modern Indian guru, a lecturer in the service of the Word. I think that that is about as far as you can get away from doing your own thing. Gay people who persevere in the desire to do their own thing usually end by doing it alone, at which point they wise up, and rely heavily in their new beginning on others! I've noticed that "do your own thing" addicts are fine until they fall in love, and do establish a relationship with someone, and then when it comes time for their lover to wander and in fact cheat, under the guise of his doing *his* own thing, they're not too happy.

Do gay lovers ever literally make vows?

I'm sure some do, but I suspect that lovers today are reluctant to tie it up that tight, and prefer tacit vows of fidelity, if any. Gay people over twenty-five have been through it before, in all likelihood, and they know that extracting a vow from a lover is to weave a web around him, to which he will react negatively. Best leave it clearly *un*said, in most cases. Where there is genuine emotion, it will survive; where there is not, it won't—a case of truth *and* consequences.

What are the special fidelity/infidelity problems of the young man/older man combinations?

Everybody's fidelity/infidelity problems are special, by the way, but a lot of them could be averted, or made less difficult, I maintain, if gay lovers grasped role-playing concepts and took on the responsibility for playing their more-than-not roles.

I have witnessed creative results from young man/older man relationships—in my own life I learned *arete* from M. In the lives of couples who fit that description, the older man is given incomparable emotional support by the younger man, who extends his belief and trust like a cup to be drunk; it is inspiriting for the mature partner. And the older man, who has succeeded in life, instructs (supports both emotionally and physically) his younger partner as the young man takes hold, learns something specific, or learns how to conduct himself in the real world efficaciously.

Their problems begin when the younger man attains strength and comprehension, and is no longer content to play a more-than-not submissive role even if that role was true and right for him at the outset of the relationship. His role may change, indeed, and the loving intimacy that used to be exists no more. If they stay together, it is under different auspices; the young man must be allowed his freedom—the chance to play the dominant role—and if he is not allowed it, he will take it, and leave his older friend, permanently.

Is it a bitter experience for the older man?

It can be, in which case the older man laments the time and trouble and money that may have been expended. But it need not be, if the older man can realize that his younger friend is not what he was, that it was time to break up, that the boy had truly gained strength, and that the new effective young man is flesh of the older man's flesh, and, in his new strength, a credit to what the older man stood for and taught.

I have seen a worse thing happen in these relationships. The younger man hangs on too long, the older man has not the guts to kick him out of the nest. They proceed along a terrible way of arguments and fights, attempting to extract a final drop of affection out of an affair that has long ago withered and died. Then, it's hell.

Or I have seen such relationships that end prematurely (especially from the older man's point of view) in which case the younger man is constantly taking the car and going off, only to return bedraggled and penniless and abandoned by some momentary lover, and time after time, the older man takes him back. Another kind of hell.

But I have also seen these relationships conclude at just about the right time, and the lovers remain friends for life—or *not end at all* but continue in supreme happiness and fulfillment for the remainder of both lives.

But isn't it the case with those last lovers you mentioned that they've arrived at some modus vivendi in the matter of infidelity?

Yes, usually—but no one either of them ever met "outside" matched what they have built and cherished in common. And invariably, they are essentially compatible in bed in their assumption of responsibility for the more-than-not roles each plays.

You mean after twenty years they can still have sex?

Indeed. You are mistaken if you don't think so. In their essential compatibility, each sees the other as he was when they first met, always. You may see two brightly dressed, overly groomed old queens—they see each other as boys grown slightly wrinkled.

What are some of the modi vivendi gay people resort to in order not to violate fidelity?

Threesomes. A person satisfactory to both lovers is picked up and brought home and is the center of a sandwich.

Also, orgies. For reasons obscure to me—but the fact of the matter—if two lovers go together to an orgy, disport themselves happily in the mishmash sex that orgies (except S & M orgies, Chapter 11) usually evolve into, it is *not* considered unfaithfulness, especially if they have at least remained in sight of one another. They can with clear consciences put on their clothes, and, refreshed and relieved, link arms and return home. They may even compare notes later, or illustrate what happened at the orgy graphically, that is to say, in action—with the two of them as the only participants.

Another method of retaining a fair facsimile of faithfulness is the one night a week each gay lover spends away from the other. This may be a spoken or unspoken arrangement. If unspoken, it is understood that the one is working late at the office, and it can be any night, *but* not more than a single night a week,: otherwise, trouble. This is exactly parallel to the "boys' or girls' night out" arrangement between heterosexual couples, and it usually works, for both straight and gay.

How do you account for two gay lovers who are eminently compatible in the ways you've described, yet still have affairs on the side?

That situation does happen. And two things facilitate it. One of the lovers (essentially compatible with his friend) suddenly sees a stranger in the street, their eyes meet, and they are off to bed at the stranger's place. I would say that the cheating lover has had an irresistible experience of beauty in the person of the stranger, which time and circumstance allow him to indulge. He comes across a perfect exterior "type" and must have union with him. When it happens, a force is loosed in the cheating lover that he feels he must succumb to or perish. My advice to such a lover is to do it and forget it, never mention his lapse to his lover whom he really does love —and try not to let it happen too frequently. That experience of beauty, which is irresistible, by the way, is one of the most mysterious and awe-inspiring in the entire homosexual galaxy of such experiences.

The second situation that may lead to "affairs on the side" between two lovers who are essentially compatible is "atmosphere," a concept I mentioned some while back and never told you about.

What is meant by "atmosphere"?

Surroundings. A terrace by the sea; a candlelit dining room; a sailing yacht running before the wind; a great house furnished with antiques; a party of people of especial conviviality. . . .

The fact is that in such surroundings, a homosexual is liable to lose his bearings. Especially susceptible to the integrity of well-made objects, to places of breathtaking breadth or width or height, to people of style—a gay person is partial to seduction in these surroundings and the fact that a long-term lover may be present is not sometimes a sufficient deterrent.

You mean the place itself or the company as a whole has some hypnotizing effect on him that contributes to an act of infidelity?

Yes. All that his long-term lover has meant to him seems to rush clean out of his mind and he falls easily into the hands of someone new and different connected with the immediate scene.

131

Surely such a labile ego must belong only to a young gay person?

Yes, mostly, but not exclusively. I have seen pairs of lovers broken up by an engaging "atmosphere" who ought to have known better. I will go into this subject of "atmosphere" and its effect on the homosexual (materialistic) sensibility in greater detail in the chapter on Palm Beach. For now, let me say that gay people (more so in the past than now), rent asunder within themselves, usually compensate for their lack of inner harmony by being irresistibly drawn to harmony outside themselves, and often make as a life's work their contribution to this exterior harmony.

In the life of a pair of homosexual lovers, isn't material inadequacy—joblessness, a dingy place to live, little money—as much a cause of infidelity as their inability to grasp role-playing concepts?

You have a point. This business of gay lovers pairing off before they have done anything to establish their careers, their material well-being, is the most troubling aspect of homosexuality for many straight people. The switching around, the seemingly endless series of brief "neurotic alliances," doesn't set well with straight people for whom stability is a watchword.

I can give you only one answer: In the life of a gay person, *love* at the beginning, *love* in the middle, and *love* at the end of his life is his most pressing consideration! Perhaps gay people would be wiser to establish themselves professionally first, but that is not the usual order of their psychological priorities. A gay person must have love to breathe, to survive from day to day! It is the nature of his homosexual nature. He must have love as an integral part of his moment-to-moment existence. I agree, too, that his definition of love has a large dollop of pure sex as the main ingredient. But love, however he conceives it—he must, or perish.

Yes, material inadequacy, the inability to create their own "atmosphere," sometimes causes so much dissatisfaction between lovers that they cannot continue a relationship once begun, and wander off from one another. On the other hand, two gay lovers in love need very little. I would ask you to recall from your own early experience at some point that, young and in love, a shared one-room apartment is a palace.

Chapter 11

S&M: A Most Dangerous Game

Is it necessary in order to develop a homosexual sensibility to know about sadistic and masochistic practices?

Yes. It is a vantage point, sufficiently bizarre and dramatic, to drive home the reality of some of what I've been describing, especially about role-playing, and it embodies at the same time all the hazards and pitfalls gay people are likely to fall into. S & M gay people are some of the best (efficacious) and worst (obsessed) in gay life. Showing you the light and dark of homosexuality is part of my goal, so that for your homosexual sensibility you may concentrate in yourself on evoking the best of it, eschewing the worst. I feel you must know about S & M; ignorance is ever the enemy.

Are S & M gay people serious about what they do?

Yes, very. On the other hand, S & M—now hear this, straight readers and gay—*is a game*. It was invented as a game by a demented, aristocratically superior personality in jail. The Marquis de Sade was an adept at self-amusement; he has provided us with the ultimate game to play, which deals in aspects of power, which he was at the time denied.

Are you saying that S & M is not to be taken seriously?

Yes, again. Some months ago I attended a weekend series of workshops called the New England Gay Conference held at Clark University in Worcester, Massachusetts (where Freud and Jung and others lectured, in the early nineteen hundreds). The most crowded workshops were two on S & M.

Students entered, took seats around a large square conference table, and they looked as if they expected instruction in the art of black magic, part of which would include the niceties of ritual human sacrifice. I found their expressions amusing. They were straining to understand in the best American tradition of doggedly "trying harder." They approached the S & M game as they would a seminar in the most abstruse philosophy; they were determined to "get it." Unfortunately, our instructor was an exhausted blimpish gay girl, and although I have been told she knows her material, that warmish afternoon she proved inarticulate, pleaded for questions from the group, received reverent stares. At the end of the workshop, there had been little knowledge imparted, and the general opinion seemed to be that it was a thorny subject, not as yet grasped. Sadistically, I wanted to shout at the disappointed conferees: *It is a game, friends, meant as an idle diversion from life, played by people of intense and often superior sensibility,* who aren't disposed toward tennis or golf, but rather toward indoor sports, and the counters in the game are not little tokens, as in Monopoly, but human relationships honed to impossible sharpness and savored with self-destructive glee. But they would have been dreadfully disappointed by my remarks so I didn't say a word. Oh, yes, I thanked the instructor for an edifying afternoon.

How is this "game," as you call it, played by gay people?

First, the conducive atmosphere is important. An isolated place is the first requirement so that one is not overheard. It

136

helps if it's dark. Accustomed to a life of dissembling in the workaday world, gay people are natural actors. Two of them are a stable unit of the game, though more can participate at orgies. One is the sadist; the other, the masochist. I am describing S & M, incidentally, as it is played by people who know what they're doing.

Can it be done otherwise?

It is mostly done otherwise.

And results in physical injury?

No, rarely physical injury, something much worse: delusion.

What is the delusion?

First, I must describe the required *illusions*, which degenerate.

All right, what are those?

Instead of speaking abstractly, let me tell you how I have played this game with consequent illusions, as S and as M. First, me as S. In a bar in Key West I met a young man, about twenty-five, who insisted upon lighting my cigarette, and who, when he had not heard something I'd said, would tilt his head appealingly and say "Please, sir?" Something stirred in my blood. I was being courted to play the game. As a conversational gesture, I clapped him on the back; he beamed. He was a nice-looking person, dark-complexioned, with soft brown eyes. He spoke little, and he seemed to advance his remarks with a tentativeness that I took as prudence, until once I interrupted him and, again, he beamed. "Go get us drinks," I snapped, throwing money on the table in the back of the bar room where he had willingly followed me. He obeyed my command. When he brought the drinks, I asked him what had taken him so long, though we both knew it had been only a minute. He said he was sorry. I felt a headiness overcome me. (Also, I was inclined to giggle, but stifled myself [in Archie's words]; if I had giggled, the boy would have been, again, disappointed. I do not like to disappoint, and fancy myself as good an actor as the next.) I informed José, as I shall call him, that when I had finished my drink, we were going to my place. He nodded his head as if that had been a foregone conclusion. We were both on target now as to the power mind-games that we would indulge in. At my pleasure, we left the bar. Jose walked just slightly behind me. Ah . . .

At my apartment, I made a show of locking the door and closing windows, and turning on the air-conditioner, which, as we both knew, would cushion the sounds of our voices. I told him to turn on the radio, get a music station, then go in the kitchen and fix two scotches, on the rocks—and be quick about it. He did these things too slowly to please me, the music station was not tuned in properly, and I ranted at his stupidity while he humbly fiddled with the radio dial. By this time we were both enchanted, wallowing in our mutual dementia: myself, proud, arrogant, punishing verbally, and absolutely in command; Jose, cringing and apologetic and subservient; he could not do enough to please me and I could not be pleased. Life for both of us was defined, we knew our places, our worth in regard to one another, our intermeshing relationship and its necessities and its boundaries: the inner persecutor objectivized! the inner weakness vilified!

Cursing him for his inferiority proven by his inability to tune the radio, while he pleaded for forgiveness and my favor, we both began to have erections. I asked him once if he was all right, and he beamed. Alternately, I continued abusing him and directing him to see to my comfort, which I never allowed him to feel he had accomplished. I began to run out of tasks for him to perform in the apartment (one must operate on a limited stage) and he had already been on his knees and scrubbed the kitchen floor, while I harangued him as to his rank incompetence at even such a simple job. Inept, stupid, dirty, I called him these names, and others. My slave begged for pity, clung to his master's knees; I stood over him as he groveled. . . . I slapped his face lightly, and he did not turn away, but clung closer and moved his face nearer my hand. This, our game, continued blissfully for two hours; actually, we had lost track of time, the symbiosis of our S & M had been so complete.

As he prepared to leave, I asked him again—"Are you all

right?" "Oh, yes," he said easily. "How do you feel?" "Like I had a mudbath," he replied contentedly. He told me he was leaving town the next day but could we get together another time. I agreed, we exchanged addresses, embraced, kissed, and he left.

I went into the bathroom; I felt drained, and satisfied, and amused. I considered my performance to have merited an Emmy at least. My face had relaxed. I remembered the sniveling, crawling, retching, defecating creature in James Joyce's *Ulysses in Nighttown*. I marveled at José's self-recognition and his superb performance.

Is that S & M?

Yes, with an emphasis on humiliation rather than ordinary discipline and physical punishment. I believe it's a finer game.

You acted out your hostility toward him, and he acted out his hostility toward himself and you were both cleansed?

Precisely.

Can you do a turnabout?

Oh, yes, every S is also an M, if the right person comes along.

What sort of person do you need? Can it be the same person?

I remember, in San Diego, a muscular submarine torpedo-man named Rocky. He smelled deliciously of engine oil. It oozed from his pores because of the body's assimilation—not because he was unclean. He was exemplary of my S's. No, it can rarely be the same person.

And how did that S & M scene go?

He was somewhat less experienced than I would have desired. I had to call the shots and execute the commands he gave me. I was, with him, director, producer, *and* actor. I worshiped his muscles and fellated him. He remained passive and unresponding until orgasm, which as the M, I enjoyed; again, a more mental type of S & M.

What about the corporeal punishment S & M scenes?

Gay people are good at them. They operate with elaborate equipment—one can buy dungeon appliances as readily these days as toasters—and they flog away with whips and chains and/or submit to handcuffs or ropes or chains or leather restraint harnesses. They also scream a lot, if the place is sufficiently isolated.

And the purpose of it?

A simple and direct expedient, and less expensive than psychoanalysis, for expiating generalized guilt, also known as original sin. But first, last, and always—a *game*. Known and treated as a game by sophisticated people, and for good results, played only by sophisticated players. José didn't look like a sophisticated individual, but he was—was he ever! He relished his role, savored it; as I relished and savored my roles with him and with Rocky. Oh, the cruel exaltation, the bittersweet pain! Dark rapture!

Why is this chapter entitled "A Most *Dangerous* Game"?

Because gay people go wrong when they think of S & M as anything more than a sophisticated game to be played out in secluded quarters. I stress it is a *game*, a mind power-ploy that has served for centuries as a useful method of mutual guilt expiation: cleansing. When S & M is lived, when it is *believed*, by either the S or the M, when the regalia is worn in the street—all that black leather and those silly caps—then the illusion of superiority on the part of the S, and the illusion of inferiority on the part of the M, degenerates into *delusion*, and the toy has become dangerous. The game is over.

So the S & M "game" mustn't get out of control?

That control, that awareness of what is going on, is *all:* a pastime for sophisticates, a toy that must be put away until the next session.

And those who let it get out of control?

Get hurt.

How?

The S by letting a cynical and tormenting attitude find its way into his out-of-bed treatment of everyone. By carrying sadistic bed attitudes and performances that work, into real life, where they do *not* work: where such attitudes bend and distort life. Finally, the S exists in a box of hate of his own manufacture, and disintegrates there, convinced of the cruelty of human nature, and the merde of living.

The M, in the same mistaken fashion, allows his sexual "kick" to become a method of coping in reality, in which case he brings down on himself his own wrath and the wrath of others. He incarnates in himself as the agent of his actual defeat, by anticipating it, by facilitating it.

In short, if the S or M is not conscious of S & M as a game, he is in trouble.

Is there an element of S & M in the conception of more-than-not dominant and more-than-not submissive role-playing?

There is. S & M is the role-playing event carried to its ultimate conclusion. But the matter of degree must be minded.

The fact that S & M exists, and, in point of fact, is becoming increasingly popular, means that dominant and submissive roles exist at a lesser level of intensity and expression, and that if one is to make an *art* of loving as a homosexual, and be successful at it, role-playing must be regarded, and understood, and paid as much heed as it deserves, but not more. Those gay people who did not comprehend their daily sex-role-playing do not comprehend S & M, and those who *do* know role-playing also know S & M, instinctively.

Would it be right to infer that there are deeper emotional circumstances and more tangled truths about homosexuality than at first meet the eye?

Perfectly right. You cannot understand the phenomenon by the melding and resisting behavior of one-celled animals as Tripp attempted to have us do in *The Homosexual Matrix*.

Do gay kids really understand S & M?

I would wish for a more articulate understanding, but I think gay kids have a feeling for S & M. I would warn them of the dangers of out-of-bed S & M attitudes. Your homosexual sensibility will be once again deepened if, with me, you catch up with what the gay kids have long been doing.

But my son! Handcuffed! Whipped! Begging for mercy!? Isn't it sick, un-American!?

For some, it is an ancient and valid and desperately essential outlet for their anxieties. Better than drugs or alcohol, almost as good as making money. S & M experts, who expiate guilt quickly and efficiently, and with care for limits, seem to me in their speed and facility to exhibit profoundly American traits.

But what about the danger of permanent physical injury?

Much less a chance of it than a chance of your car skidding off the road. Mental injury is the danger, the delusion of believing it!

Chapter 12

The Seamier Side

Don't queer hustlers abound?

Oh, you've been walking near the bus station in your city, or in certain parks, or through well-known theatrical districts, or around a particular combat-zone midtown, or along a neon-bright "strip" on the outskirts of your town—if you've been frequenting those places, yes, your impression must be that gay hustlers abound.

Aren't they dangerous psychotics?

That is the feeling about themselves that they often try to project.

Why?

It's sexy to potential customers. You wouldn't want to be out for a mad night on the town, filled with lust, and realize that the person you've picked up is a bank clerk or a ribbon sales-man or a kid away from home hard-up for change to call Dad to send cash, would you—too tame. They, those dear hustlers who stand in dark (and cold) doorways in obvious cruising places, slink or slump or strut or thrust pelvises forward or grope themselves so that you, if you're interested, can imagine that you're really getting a hot number, oblivious except for his sexual requirements, sultry, swooning with lust —which you are in a mood to satisfy. No, these are *not* dangerous psychotics. They're kids who need a buck, and haven't much idea of how to extract money from the world, and their need is always on the verge of desperation. They are harried young people whose lives will be saved if only they can get hold of twenty for . . . you name it. There are other types: kids from homes with servants and swimming pools and a social status you'd envy, who are caught up in the wildness of it, and who (like wealthy people with a small business), are more delighted with the twenty they earn hustling than with the thousand they get automatically from their trust fund every two weeks.

As you can see, I'm out to change your attitude toward gay hustlers. They are among the dearest and most ineffectual in the gay tribe—idealists to a man. Your homosexual sensibility must be brightened in regard to them. Doubtless, there are some hustlers who get in trouble, bad trouble, but they do not look for it like the members of ordinary street gangs. It is mostly forced upon them by their customers who misbehave physically or are personally insulting or refuse to keep the financial bargain. I'm sure junky hustlers can be difficult, but not murderous. The most difficult hustler is one who *poses* as a gay hustler and who is out only for cash and to vent hostility on gay people. I find this latter type a challenge to my ingenuity.

How so?

They hang out in the gay dive bars, and they attempt to con me for drinks and if they're amusing, I accede. There are usually two of them, possibly more. I remember one typical episode in Savannah, Georgia, where I had arrived en route to the Sunny South, and my beloved Palm Beach and Key West. I was tired from the day's drive, well fed by my dinner at the hotel, and curious about the local action.

A handsome boy approached me at the dive bar (which I'd located through my Gayyellow Pages), we got talking, and a friend of his also joined us. I got drunk; and they'd even bought me a round or two. Another friend of theirs joined us, more amusement: handsome and presentable boys, a little rough, and too friendly.

The conversation revolved around hustling, always a pleasant and intriguing topic. I thought at first that they were trying to ascertain my offer, and I in turn was trying to ascertain the price of the first one I had met. My suspicions of their lack of honorable intention were aroused when they left me in pairs—with one remaining behind to talk and keep me occupied—to go to the men's room. Of course, I reasoned clearly—as I do despite liquor, pills, or sorrow—they were looking for very rough action, indeed, and they were not especially gay. They would have to get me away from the bar, though, and I had to wait for the moment. Then they made their error. The three of them went together to the men's room. The second that door closed, I was up and off the premises and dashing down the street to my car.

Savannah, as you may know, is composed of a number of charming park squares, and one circumvents them via right-angled streets. As I got to the car, I spied them coming out of the bar, searching frantically for their quarry. I was one square down, in the car, started, making tracks as I saw them in the rear-view mirror racing through the square after me on foot. (I had told them I drove a Ghia.) It was like the movies, me zooming *around* the squares, tires squealing, traffic and lights be damned, and the boys fleet afoot in pursuit, *through* the squares. But my little stick-shift heavily loaded Ghia proved their match. The lights were with me at two crucial intersections. I made it to the busier part of town and back to the hotel in one piece. I thought: The day some small-town boys can con this old Bronx kid has yet to dawn. I thoroughly enjoyed a nightcap, though the hotel bartender commented that I seemed out of breath.

Doesn't that prove my point about their being psychotic?

No. I said that there were types who "pose" as gay hustlers, and I admit that that type is difficult. I described my experience to you to get that type out of the way, so we can talk about gay hustlers, whom I find mostly a delight.

In what way are they a delight?

I have rarely met a gay hustler who did not have up his sleeve the maddest scheme for getting rich quick, if only he can accumulate the cash he desperately needs to start. I know one who sent most of his daily earnings back to a peasant family in Mexico (who'd befriended him in unluckier times), so that they, and he, could start a small merry-go-round and hot-dog stand. No matter that the section of Mexico where his friends lived was mountainous, miles away from civilization or the beaten tourist paths, he was convinced that that was his ticket to fortune. I gather the Mexican family had done nothing to dissuade him. Another hustler-friend wanted money so that he could build a model of Manhattan, to scale, every single brownstone and skyscraper, to be purchased by a movie-studio scenic department for the ultimate disaster movie. (He did build some of the buildings, and his sense of scale and detail was good, I was told.) Oh, I've mentioned that gay hustlers are always temporarily down on their luck, having come (they say) from wealthy parents or having just left a wealthy sponsor. One such boy found himself penniless in Key West but resolved in his mind to make his fortune there selling fresh orange juice. He intended to squeeze the juice by hand and deliver it to the local restaurants himself on a bicycle each morning. (Also, there are hustler-kids who arrive in Key West hoping to make their fortune by selling fresh fish on street corners.) Idealists to a man, but at least *trying* to master the intricacies of the competitive system—without, however, much success. Delightful.

Are there effective hustlers?

Yes, indeed, and I will tell you about them. But no matter how effective they are, they still harbor, as a deep hope, the one fantastic scheme that will set them up for life and allow them to return home and "show" their family.

Two types of highly respectable hustlers exist. First, the loner: He advertises his services in the personal columns of various gay publications, with or without picture, always with a phone number, and his pitch is an offer to model, for camera or brush, in any degree of nudity; or to massage, his place or yours, in any degree of nudity; or to companion, by the hour, day, anywhere, in any degree of nudity. These hustlers are reliable; they do what they promise, for an agreed-upon (in advance) price. They are reliable because they are kids mostly struggling at something—students, movie-aspirants, artists of all kinds, and they have integrity, but no money and lots of "looks," and often considerable style. Also, if they do not keep promises, the publication they use will no longer accept their ad. If my life had been updated and I was young these days, I might have run such an ad. Often, the couplings that occur through the personal columns result in a relationship of ample proportions, some money, and facility therefore in whatever field the hustler may be engaged. I think, too, a prime motive of this kind of hustler may be assuagement of loneliness, and a wish for a stronger hand in his life primarily, and one that will last at the helm. He frequently succeeds.

The second, higher type of respectable hustler works through an agent by phone: price and sexual activity agreed upon and arranged in advance, via straightforward descriptions, no slipups, satisfaction guaranteed. These agents deal only with well-heeled clients, and the hustlers they handle are sophisticated. They are in it for cash, and they promise and give total, if on occasion, unusual satisfaction to their customers. They are not cold people, but rather quite dedicated and proud when they do a good job, dismayed if all does not go well, or haltingly.

I have a friend in New York who had a roommate who hustled in this manner. Let's call the roommate-hustler Sam. I had an opportunity to see the functioning of Sam's operation first-hand. Sam is a handsome young man of twenty-two, "built" as they say, though not enormously endowed sexually. And a conversational charmer: Had life deposited him in Palm Beach (the gay scene of which I shall cover in the next chapter), he would have had a rich wife in a minute, a rich male lover in two, and been the pride and joy of any social gathering. Sam dressed himself at Brooks Brothers and at Saks Fifth, mostly depending upon his customer (or "client" the word is really). He could appear as a college boy, or as a mischievous, snap-waisted, shoulder-padded European dandy or—in his white cowboy hat and superbly fashioned dungarees—as the sexually obsessed young Western hero his clients dreamed about. And talk! Sam came from the South and he could purr or chatter or snarl—to order. Some clients preferred conversation, others, "dirty-words." His descriptions of his escapades with clients—he was, when with them, studious to their needs—combined Benchley, Thurber, and Woody Allen.

One of Sam's best tales concerned his "action" with a rich client who owned a string of motels. His client would call the agent from any part of the northeast, a private plane chartered, and Sam would be flown to the city in question, driven by limousine from airport to motel, and there provided with the best suite. His client in this case, as Sam well knew, would be lurking about and observing. Sam's part was to have a cocktail at the bar and approach and seduce the bar boy (in his suite), then have dinner and approach and seduce the busboy; then have an after-dinner drink at the bar and seduce the late-duty bar boy; return to his room and call for room service, seducing each of three bellboys in succession while the client peered happily through a see-through glass mirror in the adjoining room. All arranged with the various participants in advance, of course.

Sam's role exhausted him but was not unpleasurable and he made five hundred dollars for the night's work—not to mention the trip, dinner, drinks, etc. It was part of Sam's pride, in his work, never to abuse any of the privileges that were proffered. He never overindulged or failed to leave for the other participants a tip for their legitimate services. And then, Sam would be flown back to New York, taxied to the apartment, and into the arms of my friend who owned the apartment and who turned out to be Sam's true love. Sam is the only hustler I have met who had no illusions about a get-rich-quick scheme. He took 'em as he saw 'em, and he realized that a hustler's days are numbered. He had put by a tidy sum and had many friends along the way, including myself. He looked to making financial investments and intended to retire eventually in California, to a cozy new cliff home.

What do gay people think of gay hustlers?

"There but for the grace of God go I"—or, if they're at all like Sam, "There with the grace of God shall I go!" Gay people patronize gay hustlers. It is a simple expedient when life is busy or the need is urgent. Oh, there are some snobs who've made it in terms of cash who loudly derogate their struggling brothers, but the attitude is generally permissive and amused.

Do any of the better type of hustlers make use of their opportunity for "upward social mobility"?

Yes, indeed. They are the wisest ones. They become genuinely fond of a "client" (be he old and ugly) and interested in the client's field of endeavor, and study it, and excel at it often. I have attended a testimonial dinner for one such (myself and everyone else in black-tie), and the former client extolled from the speaker's table the vast creative accomplishment of his protégé, and then the hustler expressed his appreciation for the friendship and instruction of his former client. . . . I remembered back to the days when this hustler cruised Manhattan's Third Avenue and Fifty-third Street in winter wearing a shabby old leather jacket and shoes with worn-out heels, and his price was five dollars. Such a dinner experience is edifying; one wonders sometimes if one followed the wrong road.

What is the going rate for hustlers?

That very much depends, as you can see, on the type of hustler. I understand from Sam that a "job" within city limits to which he can go and return from in a cab and which occupies no more than an hour or so of his time is worth no less than forty dollars. Sam simply tells his agent he's tired if the advance offer is not right, though Sam prides himself on his endurance (and versatility). Sam rarely "bargains." I should imagine street rates for common doorway hustlers run around twenty dollars. And if it's a snowy night, you might get it for fifteen or so. Depends, too, a bit on what you look like. If you own a VW and a Jag, do drive the Jag through the snow; the boy, even if he only gets fifteen, will warm himself and feel better in the better car, a small favor.

In other words, gay hustling follows close along the line of heterosexual hustling procedures?

I should say that the two go hand in hand. In fact, some gay agents have heterosexual clients and provide them with boys *and* girls for a delicious and varied session.

Are gay hustlers really gay?

They often protest strong heterosexual inclinations, but evidence of any current such attachment is usually hard to find.

Aren't there terrible old gay men who "use" boys and throw them out?

Yes, I guess so, but with the advent of gay lib, I find old johns are developing a jot more responsibility even toward their most casual contacts. There are also a good many boys who "use" old johns and cast them aside thoughtlessly.

What about the flippy, swishy, bleached-blond, thin, and deep-eyed queen who hangs out at a cafeteria late at night with similar cronies all obviously soliciting? Isn't theirs a low life filled with distress?

So, you've noticed. Some of them are striking if you look closely: facial features that a woman might admire, scrawny bodies that top-fashion models envy, a mien of triste decadence, despite a verbal stream of low camp. (I'll explain high and low camp in Chapter 14.) To a casual observer they look pathetic creatures, and some of them are, no doubt. But some of them are extremely provocative and mystic. Reduced in circumstance though they may be, they have also an uncanny power to calm, to mollify, even to heal others. At a time of their lives of acute sensuality, coupled with physical and mental torment, they are nevertheless possessed of a certain wholeness. It is an original kind of wholeness, childlikeness, and they are mana (giving) personalities, assuredly. Doomed to age fast, they presently flame with demonic joy and zest; keen in pleasure and steeped in sorrow; elusive, always changing, potentially violent toward themselves, evil sprites, at once beguiling and repulsive, devastating in bed and ruinous in love, sinkholes for cash, flashing cheap jewelry and decayed front teeth, dauntless and hysterical and not in the least pretending. Painted and perfumed they sit in chill chrome cafeterias, sipping tepid coffee, and telling tales of high (sexual) conquest (the seduction of their welfare inves-

tigator), raunchily. Defiant, mocking, absurd, gorgeous, helpless and beyond help—approach them warily and with awe,
keep your pity to yourself, and witness the beautiful and
damned of the netherworld of homosexuality.

Does that cover the hustler scene?

Yes, except for the gay courtesan hustlers.

What are they?

They are a special breed and would be offended at the word
"hustler." Let us say they entertain secret resources.

But they hustle?

With style, positive panache—mainly one fairly rich individual. They seem to devote themselves to his happiness. But
let me limn Stephen. He is blond, about twenty-three, he is
dressed too exquisitely (decked in gold jewelry), and he drives
his own new Triumph. He lives with his older friend, Ralph, a
successful businessman. Ralph dotes on Stephen, and with
reason. In bed, Stephen exhibits a sensitivity and care to his
older lover's needs that is, well, incomparable. And out of
bed, Stephen is equally supportive. If Ralph is depressed,
Stephen knows it and with a caress or a kind laugh or a moment of intense sympathy, sometimes unspoken, he can pull
Ralph's world back together.

Ralph is not only enamored, he is transfixed by Stephen.
He objects only to Stephen's sudden and afterward unex-
plained absences, and trinkets on Stephen that he did not
buy. In their five years together, Ralph has learned from
Stephen to be satisfied with what he gets, which, as I said, is
considerable. But Ralph throws tantrums especially at the
sight of a new watch, necklace, or bracelet.

About Stephen's absences. He has a circle of clandestine
friends, three or four, one of whom is famous, all richer than
Ralph—but not so easily manipulated, yet. Stephen keeps
them lined up (kneading them slowly into shape) until the day

arrives when he can no longer tolerate Ralph's tantrums, and, without a word, he will depart—to one of them. Since he is growing older daily, as Stephen is cruelly aware about himself, he will stay with whichever of the new lovers he has best trained to his style of life, love and absence. He will repeat his pattern of clandestine friendships, including sentimental clandestine reunions with Ralph. Do not mistake Stephen —he hustles, but he gives ample measure for goods and cash received. It's just that he can't resolve his conflict. If he involves himself in a job, he will grow old; if he grows old, he will no longer be lovable; if he is unlovable and old, he cannot live well; if he can't live well and be loved, he'd rather die.

Stephen ineffectually attempts suicide. It is Ralph he calls at the last minute, and it is Ralph who rescues him (ambulance, stomach pump, etc). Stephen figures his physical and mental recovery period in Ralph's tender care should be worth at least another two years; Ralph is delighted. But one day Stephen disappears briefly again, returns home without explanation, etc., etc., etc.

Chapter **13**

The Super-Rich Gay Scene

Will my developing homosexual sensibility be substantially advanced by knowledge of the "super-rich gay scene"?

No, not substantially, but subtly. In this chapter you will achieve a perspective on what is clearly the *materialistic homosexual sensibility*, more for your diversion than anything else.

Do you mean by the chapter heading that we are to hear about gay people who, themselves, are super-rich?

No, I mean to describe the life of certain gay people who frequent the super-rich scene, in particular, Palm Beach, Florida.

Why Palm Beach?

Because Palm Beach is mecca to the super-rich, and to gay people of materialistic sensibility. Also, I am a Palm Beach "buff."

What about San Francisco, Dallas, Detroit?

No, I hate to tell you, but social eyes turn to the East for final directions. I would include as suburbs of Palm Beach the town of Bar Harbor, Maine; Fishers Island, New York; Newport, Rhode Island; Southhampton, Long Island; and a few other scattered municipalities like New York's East Side and Nantucket Island, Massachusetts—but the real action on this continent occurs in Palm Beach—for American socialites. And for the gay "little brothers" of the super-rich.

You mean if a gay person has been involved in Palm Beach with Palm Beachers, he has achieved a certain distinction?

Yes, absolutely.

What is the distinction?

In subjecting himself to life in Palm Beach, he has encountered in the most dramatic fashion every difficulty and every positive value in regards to his materialistic homosexual sensibility that he can possibly encounter. If he has a dime's worth of brains, he has the opportunity to become a very sophisticated gay person.

What are the component characteristics of this materialistic homosexual sophisticate?

He is on no account self-deluded or fooled. He has realized down to his Guccis that money makes this Palm Beach world go round. Love is a negligible commodity, easily bought. To be pertinent here, one must be very, very rich. Without pots of money, to be regarded at all, one must have a useful talent. But let me describe him in person, as a man of about thirty-five.

Freshness of grooming, dress, demeanor, are the things that strike you. Without straining, he has preserved a youthful naturalness; he walks with ease and his eyes are merry and his voice always humorful and concerned, but not overly. He seems to have found the most exquisitely balanced midpoint of everything! If he has a single excess, it is in the expression of a positive and hopeful attitude about everything! Oh, and he may wear a bit too much good jewelry.

He plays golf and tennis and bridge. He knows that the valued quality of a Rolls-Royce is the fact that it is so quiet, that it preserves, while riding, the continuity of a human relationship and consequent conversation, begun on the golf course or poolside or at dinner, and he knows that human relationships, enjoyment of them, extraction from them of the last drop of mutual appreciation, is *the* point. He is exhilarated by the mere existence of beauty: in women, in men, in landscapes, in weather conditions, and in himself. He wants to be beautiful in every action and in every thought; though he may not always succeed with the latter, he never fails with the former.

Since he is at best only moderately well off, he "does" something in Palm Beach—contributes to the creamy, pastel-smooth "atmosphere" of that most perfect world. He has an art gallery or an antique shop or a flower shop or a boutique, or he designs women's clothes or the interiors of vast houses, or, in a pinch, he "does" hair (a far more honored profession than one might think, especially in Palm Beach where women never appear casually; the pay is considerable, and the fringe benefits of personal association with one's employer and travel benefits and equal personal accommodations at home or abroad are also considerable).

He dances in his black patent-leather pumps with assuredness and rhythm, and he always sees to it that the most cumbersome dowager present is waltzed about the floor at some point during the evening. He has a witty remark and an appreciative one ever on the tip of his tongue. He receives an accolade with shy grace or with such amusing hyperbole that the compliment is absorbed as just and rejected as undeserved—in the same moment.

He is capable of heterosexual sex when it is most urgently required of him: to restore the amour propre of some lady rejected in promiscuous love—or by her dull and golf-obsessed millionaire husband—and he is past master at compensating for passion by delicate touches and suggestions of manly submissiveness in bed.

He is a bearer of small and appropriate gifts, a steady

155

stream. Also, he sends the correct floral tributes to the correct person at the correct time. Flowers have a special message and must be designated for special missions, not squandered unless it is for a particularly ebullient lady giving an especially large party. Parties! He attaches the invitations he receives daily with a stapler into the pages of a large book and mentally winnows the ones he will accept from the ones he will charmingly and by note of hand decline. He is partial to parties, and the names of the socialites of world renown, as hosts or fellow guests, or the titles of even minor royalty, thrill him with the same lusty excitement that a fan of the Chicago Bears feels when his team comes on the field. He is sharply aware of the social protocol of the world in which he lives (and in which he draws every breath with fanatic rapture). It is his study of a lifetime to really know whose word at a party is to be paid heed, whose to be privately discounted; which among the attendant luminaries are the highest stars in the social firmament though not exceedingly rich and which are the beggars though billionaires who can never hope to touch them, or even talk to them except in passing.

He knows himself to whom he can properly address a remark, and from whom he may admit a remark or a joke. He is generous and kind to other gay people in a circumstance roughly parallel to his own, but he does not notably consort with them, nor avoid them either. He is scrupulously fair in his conduct with those less well acquainted with the scene, gay or not, but he is capable of a searing if unobtrusive and quite merrily voiced, utterly destructive remark.

He has himself faced social disapprobation. There is always one great lady in the bunch who is of high quality even in his eyes, but who nevertheless displays a blatant suspiciousness in regard to him and won't have him in her sight. She has long been his nemesis; she has no proof for her innuendos, and as long as she does not, he is safe and he is defended by his friends of her equal rank who are unbelieving or unconcerned or tacitly agreed that he is a presentable person and what he really is or does privately doesn't matter. But he also knows *this:* Should he reveal his homosexuality "in the street, and disturb the horses," as it were, his great lady nemesis would take the offensive against him with implacability and she would sway friend and foe and lesser and greater and, *without* a torchlight manhunt—*but* in ways similarly grim and violent—hunt him down and destroy him, shred him to bits,

and throw his carcass to the dogs. And he knows this, too:
Once such an event has occurred, there is no reinstatement,
no forgiveness though he be the most talented of all talents in
his field; he is finished in Palm Beach and in every place Palm
Beachers go; he might as well die. Perhaps it is this knowledge that makes the prize he holds so dear, dear enough to
sacrifice, except on occasions of most pressing need, the
expression—to any degree—of his homosexuality in public.
On those rare forays he takes in pursuit of sexual fulfillment,
he goes his way accompanied by drumbeats of the social death
march, and a sadness in his eyes that bespeaks his danger and
his desire. One slip, and it is ended. He slides, the rungs of
the ladder of his ascent torn from his hands, to the bottom and
the hell, holy and fierce and unending, of ostracism: an empty
mailbox, a silent phone, himself considered invisible.

**Under those totally threatening circumstances, what is
his gay sex experience, if he should allow himself to
have any?**

If he is a loner, his experience in love is brief, and usually
drunken and anonymous. If by chance he has arrived in Palm
Beach with a longtime lover, and they have cohabited and
attempted to go about in society, they are condemned to the
lower levels of it, never to rise very high. Oh, how they wait
for the "best" invitations, which never come.

And if he is exposed as a homosexual?

He is out. Though he may retain one friend.

Who is that?

Often the woman who was his original sponsor, provided she
is herself most secure. She is the lady who in his heyday might
have remarked (though *not* in reference to him), "I enjoy gay
people. They're fun, interesting, good to look at. My best
friends are gay . . . they're truer than women, reliable—and
just being with them makes me feel better. They emanate

vitality, a passion for life . . . I get a spiritual charge when I'm with my gay friends. I love to see life as they see it. Of course they're talented and of course there's a homosexual sensibility . . . in books, theater, the design of my clothes, my home. I share their sensibility . . . I couldn't live without it. . . ." This great lady, in spite of all, will still receive a disgraced homosexual, though mostly to her more intimate parties, or vis-à-vis.

Is this sort of individual an admirable person?

He is to me, though I could not or would not be like him. He has dedicated himself to the materialistic homosexual sensibility, rendered so keenly sensitized by his P.B. surroundings. . . . I admire his tacit resolve to give up everything and anything that might stand in his way of experiencing it. His life has been tuned to a fine pitch; he has made of his sensibility the highest art. He has become almost a eunuch in its service. Nothing gives him greater ecstasy than its visual fulfillment.

Hasn't he been "taken in" a bit about what is important in life?

You mean like family and security and good friends? From your point of view, and mine, somewhat, yes. But from his, we're the fools who exist simply to service—in one way or another, and no matter how remotely—the world he so adores. He views us, I'm afraid, as the masses.

What do the super-rich see in him?

The husbands see not much, unless his "service" (shop) is useful, or his art gallery openings are amusing and with plenty of free drinks.

Do the super-rich care about free drinks?

It's amazing, but they do, in the right circumstances, of course. They adore cadging a free drink or a free buffet, right alongside our gay friend who enjoys it also. It's faddish, at the moment, for certain super-rich people to run a business (in Palm Beach), and the few pennies they actually earn, as I've mentioned before, give them gleeful pleasure.

What, essentially, do the super-rich women see in gay people?

I've told you what the sponsor of the man I've been delineating said, about the reward of her association generally with gay people. I think probably her gay friends serve her best as *escorts*. Gay men have not forgotten—as her dullard husband has most often—how to dance and laugh and, yes, play. It has been said that people are most human when they are at play. I think gay people always remember how to play, and that the super-rich ladies whom they escort appreciate that. Her husband knows that her escort is gay, and he feels no challenge. It's a bit insulting to the gay person, but there it is. Everyone benefits.

But aren't these gay frequenters of the Palm Beach scene really out for the money, one way or another?

No, they are not. And anyway, the money, as you rightfully refer to it, is so wrapped up and guarded by banks, lawyers, relatives, and ugly watchdog type friends that very few ever find their "way" to it. Let me be very bold: Besides the fulfillment of the requirements of his materialistic sensibilities, I think, in general, a gay person attracted to Palm Beach (all right, I'll include Hobe Sound and Boca Raton) finds a gorgeous "symmetry" in the style of the people and in the environment, compensating perhaps for the lack in him of an inner symmetry, by which he comes closest to a primitive conception in himself of . . . God. That is the only explanation I can find that suits me as to the intense devotion these certain gay people evince for the Palm Beach scene.

Aren't there "for real" young men kept by these super-rich women?

Some, but not as many as you might think. Oh, these ladies might take a fling once in a great while with a young climber who'd managed the proper introductions, but the ladies are expert in spotting a person who is merely a gigolo (as gay people on the scene are not, since they offer some product or service). And though the climber might spend a pleasant month, or even a season, in P.B., he is usually dispensed with. If the rich lady doesn't do it, her nasty watchdog friends will. I enjoy the sight of a typical and hard-to-beat ploy to get rid of a climber. The lady, subtle and graceful and wise, suddenly begins to act quite nutty, her conversation becomes dissociated and her behavior eccentric, and the climber takes to his heels.

Are there super-rich gay men?

Yes, but if they indulge at all, it is in another country.

Never in Palm Beach?

At their peril. I did know one man who . . .

Please tell—who, what?

Just gossip, but then, as Jacques Barzun informs us, what is culture *except good gossip* down through the ages about how to live! So I'll tell you about "Charlie Strong," his downfall.

I was between literary projects one season, not so long past, and I needed a job, and I found myself applying for one in an elegant Palm Beach antique shop. I had sold antiques (refurbished capstans and hawser blocks) one year at a well-known New York store, and I had therefore some experience. I was hired, in Palm Beach, by Charlie Strong, who owned the shop, and that was how I was in a position to know what happened. He told me.

Charlie Strong had come from a good midwestern family; he'd had a desultory education and drifted about. Charlie's goals were two: satisfy a powerful gay sex drive, and an even more powerful drive—to be rich. He joined the Navy before World War II and wangled a commission. In those days he cut the finest figure of a young man: tall, dark, wide-eyed, with a mellifluous voice and impeccable manners—and stunning in his naval officers' whites. He personified the gay materialistic sensibility I've described.

At a tea in Newport, Rhode Island, given for the men in service by a dowager in residence in one of the great mansions there, he met an heiress, whom we'll call Nita—a very shy and confused woman, despite her wealth—who took a shine to him. Charlie saw his chance and he grabbed it, besides which he had an opportunity to be helpful to this lady, ten years his senior, by bolstering her ego with love, and he did. They were married, and moved to her forty-room "beach cottage" in Palm Beach. Nita was more super-rich than Charlie had imagined: many properties around the country and around the world and an abundance of cash. Her "social" heritage was unbeatable. That had been thirty-odd years ago, and Charlie had reigned in Palm Beach as the shah of fun (because he specialized in parties with Persian motif) for the last ten of it. (He had struggled for his social "place" for the first twenty-odd years, and Charlie's rise had been comparatively quick.) When I walked into the shop, which he ran for "fun," Charlie had reached the last rung in the ladder he'd climbed for social acceptance—he had only to perch himself on the top. But he fell off, in his late sixties, before my very eyes.

Palm Beach is an island in a bay, joined to the town on the mainland across from it, West Palm Beach, by drawbridges. (Palm Beachers plan, "come the revolution" which they guiltily and horrendously anticipate, to simply raise those bridges.) West Palm Beach is really just a service town for P.B. The live-out servants live there, and P.B.ers passing through on their way to the airport customarily pull the shades in their limousines. West Palm Beach has three very well decorated gay bars, especially one I shall call the Surf West. Although I have mentioned that real P.B.ers, the gay ones, cruise at their peril, the parking lot at the Surf West is nightly, during the season, in the wee hours, jammed with Rolls and Mercedes, and evening-jacketed older gay society people, usually drunk out of their minds and fresh from some Palm Beach soirée, can be seen ducking out of their cars and into the bar. Charlie Strong was often in attendance—his social position was inviolable, he thought. And as a matter of fact, his "incident" did not occur in the bar, but later, heading home, as he steered his maroon Mercedes convertible unsteadily toward one of the bridges.

He picked up a young man who was thumbing a ride. He brought the young man to Palm Beach, and right to the "cottage." Nita had adjourned to a local hospital for her biyearly checkup (she was almost eighty but still perky), and it was Thursday, the servants' night off. Charlie believed he'd managed privacy. He gave the young man a drink and sat down on a couch beside him.

Now before I tell you the upshot, I must explain about P.B. police, a specially trained cadre. Unless there has been a murder, they try never to arrest a Palm Beacher. The police see themselves, rightly, as rather keepers of the peace and soldiers of order. If a P.B.er is in trouble, they attempt to help. Usually, they provide the P.B.er with a ride home, if he is on foot, or with a police car escort to the driveway, if he is mobile, and especially if the P.B.er is driving and drunk. The young man Charlie Strong gave a ride to in West Palm Beach happened to be an off-duty Palm Beach cop, who observed Charlie's free-form driving, and in a gesture of helpfulness thumbed a ride and intended to see to it Charlie got safely home and tucked in bed, an actual police service that is often rendered.

On the couch with this young man, Charlie made distinct overtures. The cop was not unfamiliar with it and suggested that Charlie retire forthwith. Charlie slugged the young man hard, in the face. The young cop produced his credentials, Charlie slugged him again. The cop, now bleeding from the mouth and eye, called the station house. Charlie was arrested and locked up, so drunk he had no idea what had happened, except that the young policeman's blood covered his white ruffled shirt front.

Nor did he wake up in his cell the next morning before the P.B. radio and TV were grinding out each half hour the report of Charlie's "assault on a policeman, and lewd and lascivious behavior." Nita saw the report in her hospital room. Everyone in P.B. saw it. Storm clouds gathered that morning, and by afternoon the storm had burst.

I must interject this: Charlie had enemies—people of less social rank and distinction and much less amusing. They were jealous. Although Palm Beachers had feted at Nita and Charlie Strong's parties for almost four decades, although Charlie himself had proffered the proper introduction to many a young man who had thoroughly entertained a dowager, and although Charlie had provided for the rich old-boys many a pretty face to sit beside at dinner (later beside the old-boy in bed), when the issue, the specter of homosexuality, threatened, the moral dignity of Palm Beach disgorged itself like a golem, and smote Charlie dead. Nita drew their compassion.

Released on bail in his own cognizance, Charlie left jail but he could not go home. Nita had instructed her servants literally to pack two bags of Charlie's clothes and to meet Charlie at the driveway gate of her cottage and hand them over when Charlie came. The house itself was bolted and barred and Nita's lawyer hired four men with watchdogs to patrol! Under an assumed name—but known to the merest desk clerk as the social celebrity he was—Charlie checked into the Breakers. He had to ask the hotel for credit; they agreed to carry him for a week.

This occurred toward the end of the season in P.B. when I was still working for Charlie at the shop. He called the shop, but its board of directors, who had enjoyed the "fun" of imagining they had some say in the shop's affairs (Charlie's wit to include them) had actually taken over the running of it and forbade Charlie to appear there or to phone. When I picked up the phone once, it was Charlie, and he asked me to meet him and of course I did. Meanwhile, the scandal had spread wildly, and people who had entered the shop for years and loved Charlie now stopped by only to denounce him: queer, obscene old man, they despised him, and pitied Nita. Nita's relatives came in a body and instructed his longtime employees (who were also friends) not to see Charlie or talk to him or accept any communication from him if they wanted their jobs. The relatives and board of directors had applied to law to buy Charlie out quite cheaply, and the case would be tried in a few days.

Charlie had one friend left, a very great lady, whom in jest he had called the Queen of Palm Beach and who, in fact, because of her charm and reality, had, indeed, become the Queen of Palm Beach. We met at her house. In one of those twists of fate that occur at imperative moments, Charlie saw me as a connection with the shop which he loved, and after plying me with questions about activities there, he confided in me.

He said that he didn't know what had happened with the policeman, but that he was certain the affair did not happen as it had been described. Nita, at almost eighty and after having been married to Charlie all those years, continued to be out to his calls, and to deny him entry to the house. Her lawyer had informed him she'd filed for divorce and struck Charlie from the will, and also sold off properties away from Palm Beach of which Charlie had been fond. Surrounded by her relatives, lawyers, and commiserating friends, Nita was adamant. Charlie told me that he would deny everything in court, about the alleged assault, that he would fight the board of directors about the shop, and that "they" were persecuting him not because of the incident, but because "they" were jealous. He said to me if only people—his old friends!—would stop gossiping, the whole thing would blow over, *it always had*. I realized then that the gossip I had heard about Charlie's other gay incidents had basis. I saw Charlie plain. He used the only super-rich technique he knew for dealing with trouble: deny it, ignore it, rise above it like a bubble. It had worked for him all his adult life; he believed it would work then; it didn't, Charlie had fallen, but his story had a happy ending of sorts.

I left Palm Beach after speaking to Charlie, but here's what happened: The police charge was sustained in court and Charlie was fined and given a probationary period. The shop's board of directors succeeded in wresting the shop from him for a pittance—*his* shop. Except for the Queen, not one of his friends supported him. They hacked him verbally into social oblivion; on the street he was invisible. He moved from the Breakers to a small motor inn in West Palm Beach. He began to slip mentally and not know where he was. He tried to go home and the dogs snapped at him through the driveway gate. In spite, Nita had even sold that Palm Beach "cottage"—in which she'd been born!

But then a curious thing occurred. Nita, whose life with Charlie had been a full one and a merry one for almost forty years, and whose life without Charlie was inconceivable, did a turnabout.

I like to imagine it this way: still in her great mansion, Nita in bed suddenly waking before dawn and sitting straight (she held herself in a stiffly proper posture). I picture her saying to herself: I've lived with the man for almost forty years, I've known he was gay. He gave me the best of himself and saw to it that I had the best he could give. I loved him and he loved me. At this point she rings for the servants, tells them to pack up (and out) her relatives in the guest rooms; she phones and fires her lawyers and dismisses the wicked house guards and their dogs; she tells the world to go to hell and asks, "Where's Charlie?!"

They did get back together, that genuinely aristocratic old lady with her honorable heart, and poor disgraced Charlie. It was too late to save the Palm Beach cottage or any of the other properties or the shop. Charlie and Nita traveled extensively after that. I read recently that Nita had died in her sleep in New York, and I heard that Charlie had taken the directorship of an elegant health spa in Tasmania.

Chapter 14

Camp Humor

Didn't Susan Sontag offer an authoritative definition of camp humor?

She did, and close to the mark, as I remember. She explained it, and suddenly the kind of humor I have been exposed to and enjoyed most of my life, and frequently indulged in, became a high intellectual precept.

This lifting up to a "chilly pinnacle" of something that used to be warm and useful in my life has occurred once before. Two and a half decades ago in Key West, I worked as a waiter in a restaurant that occupied a historical mansion. (I set down my experiences of the era in a novel, *The Last of the Southern Winds*.) The old mansion, called the Caroline Lowe House, was subsequently abandoned, and burned partly and was finally razed. But the Key West Historical Society saved a notable feature of the mansion: a particularly handsome section of the main staircase, the newel-post and eight or ten steps, and this item is on display in the local memorabilia collection at an old Key West fortress. I can remember taking "tricks" up that very staircase (running my hand over the newel-post) to an assignation in my third-floor room under the eaves, and other employees there at the time did the same thing. Can you imagine! What had been the merest adjunct to my sex life is now a celebrated and treasured museum exhibit!

I feel very much the same thing has happened to "camp" humor. The distinct, ironic point of view of gay people, which elicited their gales of laughter, has now come into the public domain as a polished method of perception of life. As I am pleased about the fortune of that section of staircase —available for everyone's enjoyment though not the same as mine—I am pleased that camp humor has become an object of serious consideration for thinking people, which is not the use I made of it, but what the hell!

What use did gay people make of camp humor?

Oh, it was a sort of secret gay people shared that made them laugh, and recognize one another.

Can that idea be elucidated?

Yes. Haven't you ever been in a situation that was puzzling to others because they did not know the motivation of all parties concerned—while you did, and couldn't reveal it? Weren't you a touch superior to those struggling for comprehension and amused by their attempts to understand? Camp humor devolved out of that situation, or one similar to it: the emotional position of gay people in a straight world. Gay realism in contrast to straight reality. Not that the unknown factor of every conundrum was homosexuality, but that the world was not quite as it appeared to be. Those, straight and gay, who took life at face value and believed everything everybody else believed could not participate in camp humor.

Isn't camp humor cruel and cutting, as during a gay "bitch fight"?

I haven't seen or rather heard a gay "bitch fight," as you call it, in many a day. I suppose these fights occur, but not much anymore. Or I don't go to the right places! Bitch fights seem to me to be of a different genre: the humor of insult school, so deftly exercised in the past by Milton Berle, and these days by Mr. Lovable: Don Rickles. No, that humor is different.

What, then, *is* camp humor?

I make a distinction that others have made, dividing camp humor into "low" camp and "high" camp.

What is "low" camp?

Ironic perception, plus outrageousness.

For instance, there is a bartender at the Boatslip whose nickname is Parky. He is a hat queen. One afternoon he arrived on the job wearing a fluggy cheap wig styled in the manner of the 1940s, and a little heart-shaped pale-blue satin hat with one fake flower of the same material and hue jutting forward from it. I had seen such a hat, as perhaps you have, worn by women of the period in perfect earnest. It is hilarious now as a detail of garb, and frankly, to gay people, such a hat would have been hilarious when it was fashionable. It is and was such a naïve expression of sexual desire—the flower awaiting, courting the bee to fertilize it (though an articulation of that gesture would probably not have been made). Gay people—sensitive to psycho-sexual motivation—quickly discern the pathos and hopeless yearning of that hat.

A famous bit of low camp humor came out of the beat generation, as exemplified by Allen Ginsberg, who sat in a subway car reading a newspaper with a hole torn in the middle through which he peered at his fellow travelers, much to their discomfort. He had injected low camp humor into an everyday situation; made a parody of a man reading a newspaper on the subway.

Another example of low camp: A world-famous novelist of my acquaintance with whom I was dining—along with others in a restaurant—suddenly stood up and screamed: "All lesbians out!" You can picture the consternation in that dining room. I won't explain that one; it was just funny, although probably not to any lesbian who might have been there. Low camp. Pure outrageousness.

Can you give examples of "high" camp?

Yes, high camp is not a belly laugh as low camp frequently is; it is funny but the joke takes longer to evolve, and it is based on a capital irony. A capital irony derived, I am bound to say, from the projection into the world of *someone's fantasy passing for real*. The joy of it for gay people is the sight of others taking it seriously. Incidentally, camp may contain its high and low aspects in the same moment.

Examples?

Mary Hartman, Mary Hartman, was the best example. An ironic soap opera, the program was clearly a parody of manners and mores of the sort of TV fare adored by ironing housewives in the afternoon. The fantasy of *Mary Hartman, Mary Hartman* became so outrageous that it convinced! The program's writers even went so far as to enlist Gore Vidal as a participant! The joy of it was to see this long joke evolve, episode by episode, till credulity was strained, broken, mended again!

Since I am a writer, literary examples of high camp rush to mind, involving homosexuality. Proust's seven-volume novel, *Remembrance of Things Past,* the work of a master prose artist, is nevertheless a thorough explication of the homosexual sensibility. It is well known that Proust used boy models for his female characters and didn't even bother to change the names much: Albertine for Albert, etc. Also, in the last volume, a number of the important male characters turn out to have been, or become, homosexual. A long and well-told camp, as it has been described by others than myself.

Even Ernest Hemingway tried his hand at camp. His novel *Torrents of Spring,* presented seriously, is a parody of Sherwood Anderson, to whose fluffy and soulful prose Ernest objected. I don't mean to imply either one of them was gay, or that all parodies are homosexually initiated or oriented. In this case, the method of high camp, puncturing by exaggeration someone's fantasy passing for real, was adopted. Ernest's joke was on the reader, who, again, took it seriously. Hemingway's pose of utter masculinity, which he fostered amusedly, then took seriously himself, is another instance of high camp, according to those who knew him in the early days.

Speaking of someone's fantasy passing for real as an aspect of high camp, take Bette Midler. Gay people as well as straight love that tacky, clumsy broad whose dauntless spirit triumphs over her seeming lack of talent; gay people of a certain kind see themselves exemplified in her efforts. She seems rarely to get anything right—which is her deliberate art—but when she does, it is moving. She strikes a strong chord in gay bumblers. Phyllis Diller preceded her at this. The list is long. The great women of the stage and screen, whose fantasies pass for real, include Mae West, Tallulah Bankhead, Joan Crawford, and of course Bette Davis. Besides projecting their splendid and vigorous fantasies, they are, to a woman, defiant souls, and gay people have appreciated that quality in them. High camps, all, and widely acknowledged (among gays) as such.

High camp is still not clear. Can it be made clearer?

Probably not. I am up against what every interpreter of camp humor has been up against: your lack of familiarity with the homosexual sensibility *as it is lived*. In this book, I hope that at least to some extent you have become more familiar with it and its special slant. And enjoyed—in the widest sense—the uniqueness of it. And have adapted some of its ways and means and insights for yourself. But to understand camp humor is, in the end, to know the world from the ironic point of view, deeply ingrained, of that sensibility. Not to have lived it, as, presumably you have not, is to be handicapped as to the finer points of camp humor, although straight people have certainly grasped it and made it their own in broadest outline, for which I'm glad.

How would one go about sharpening a sense of camp humor?

Keep an eye out for obvious ironies: the difference between the way things ought to be and the way they are. Solid American idealistic government? Witness Watergate and the sex scandals in Congress! Rectitude in business? For the want of a jet cargo door redesign, three hundred passengers died in a crash. Then watch for subtler ironies: Ex-Secretary of Agriculture Butts, a bastion of authority, making jokes about blacks. Ex-President Ford, who ought to know, telling us that Eastern European countries are *not* Soviet-dominated.

Are gay people prone to "put on" straight people?

Yes, in certain circumstances the temptation is great, and it is acceded to now and again. I had a kidder at a job one time who constantly queried me about my sex life, attempting to put me down. One day I decided to "have at" him. I proceeded (in the john where the salesman rested and gabbed) to invent a sex life for myself as a heterosexual with the most elaborate and obscene descriptions. The kidder's mouth dropped open, the others stared. I have no idea whether or not he believed me, but his kidding stopped. And then, there are people, straight and gay, who do *so* believe in the world as they see it that the temptation to "play in" to their delusions is overwhelming: to goad them on in their naïveté and prejudice.

Gay people can be puckish?

Can be. But there is often a point to their puckishness that is not uncreative. Driven by bland reasoning or argument to some extreme position, the individual goaded on by a puckish gay person sometimes begins himself to see the error of his perceptions, and revises them. It's called "giving a man enough rope . . ."

Is the gay person always right?

Absolutely.

And that last exchange of Q.&A. is an example of camp?

It is, you're getting it.

How much of Straight Answers is camp?

Far less than I would have wished. At first, I'd intended to make it high camp indeed. But when I actually sat down to write, I felt a persistent and realistic responsibility to you and to the subject matter, and it became clear that a book-long relationship with you that was entirely camp would not serve my purpose, so it simply did not come out that way. Although I am aware some gay people may disagree; their reasoning goes like this: "Oh God, Miss Loovis has been scribbling again! What's that mad queen dishing about this time?"

Was your previous book, *Gay Spirit*, camp?

Yes, except that toward the middle of it, I began to, again, feel more responsibility toward my gay audience than I'd planned, and so the book, commenced as a spoof of all of those heterosexual sensuous "manuals," ended up with some serious things to say about gay life as I see it. This transition from a comic work to a serious work combined in a single effort is not unfamiliar. Jean Marsh, the writer of (and actress in) the TV series *Upstairs, Downstairs*, told on an interview program how she had begun the story of the Bellamys as a joke, and intended it as a travesty. Viewers took it seriously, and Jean Marsh reoriented her objectives.

To a large extent, then, camp exists in the eye of the beholder?

Yes, well put. Addison Mizner's Spanish palace architecture in Palm Beach was his idea of designing grand places to live. (He got so wrapped up in his idea that he sometimes forgot staircases and bathrooms right through the construction stage of the house.) The houses are certainly impressive, symbols of old P.B., if you happen to have enough money to own one, but too big and airy to effectively air-condition, and ditto to heat, in constant need of repair (especially the tile roofs), and requiring a platoon of servants to operate, who, even for the super-rich, are hard to find. Such houses today are a camp, in the eye of this beholder, and in the opinion of present-day architects in the area. I'm certain, however, that few of the owners think so. Dear, recently deceased Marjorie Merryweather Post owned the largest of Mr. Mizner's creations in Palm Beach; she couldn't find a buyer, and she had a hard time convincing even the United States Government to take it over, free.

Then, if not cruel, is camp humor mainly derisive?

No. It does not contain the purely derisive quality of what used to be called "the Bronx cheer." It reveals, I think, *an affectionate indulgence of fantasy*—conscious that a particular camp is the result of someone's fantasy passing for real. But camp humor is also conscious of the fact that *certain fantasies are well constructed*, to be appreciated on that count. And then maybe, in the words of Peggy Lee's plaintive song: "That's all there is, my friends."

Gay people, because of their life-style, are peculiarly equipped with a camp sense of humor?

Yes, exactly. To be homosexual in this country at this time, in business especially, is to be forced to live a life of dissembling, as I've mentioned to you before. *I* know what the reality of being gay is, but my business colleagues rarely know, or will rarely admit knowing, which amounts to the same thing. So in order to be allowed to earn one's living, one tries to say as little as possible about oneself personally, but temptation arises—to "invent" a heterosexual existence for others' consumption (as I've described), and then to have fun with the whole thing, in one's own mind, to alleviate boredom. If one is exposed often enough to the need to appear just "one of the boys," one learns how, and then one learns to savor the ironies between one's appearance and one's realities.

The addition of a camp sense of humor to your evolving gay sensibility will provide you with a new and constant source of merriment.

I am aware that the gaiety of a gay person has, sometimes, a terribly frivolous sound for worldly ears, and seems the more preposterous as coming from people whose outward circumstances are often of the most uncomfortable kind. I think this rich strain of ironic humor is a psychic saving grace for gay people, who have learned steadfastness and patience in the face of suffering. Their mirth persists through every hardship and tribulation. Morose resignation for gays? Never! Shock the world by a delicate playfulness in spite of all—absolutely!

Chapter 15

Politicizing Our Passions: Gay Lib

What is the "thrust" of the gay lib political movement?

To have unfair sodomy laws—unfair in that these laws are selectively enforced against homosexuals while *all* are guilty—revoked on the books of state legislatures. To be replaced with laws forbidding discrimination against homosexuals in any area: jobs, housing, right to assemble, etc. Also, on a national level, some sort of similar though broader legislation with the same purpose.

Are gay individuals dedicated to this "thrust" in sufficient numbers to be called a "movement"?

You are suggesting that the gay lib movement is a media event. I suspected as much, too, until I began to look into the subject. It is not a media event. As a matter of fact, a great deal of what is going on is not reported by the straight media, as it is by the many gay magazines, newspapers, radio stations, club bulletins, and an occasional TV presentation. There are more than a handful of gay organizations in any city of fair size. There are individuals who have come to feel that political proselytizing is the thing they can do best for gay lib and they do it. Behind them, mute perhaps but in sympathy, stand many millions of people, gay and straight, who've come to realize that the persecution of gay people is most particularly bound up with human rights. The homosexual liberation movement cuts across every social and ethnic grouping, and it is a persecution that goes back for millenniums, not centuries. The day after the Supreme Court refused to hear an appeal of Virginia law that proscribed homosexual activity even between consenting adults in private, therefore tacitly upholding that law in Virginia and in other states, the staid old Boston *Herald* ran an editorial entitled "Retreat on Rights," which ended with these words: "Under our system, any court decision, however unpalatable, is binding and must be obeyed. But we cannot help wondering whether, in the constant struggle between liberty and order, liberty is losing ground." *The New York Times* ran a similarly slanted editorial piece. Oh, yes, there is a gay lib movement, a very active one.

Why doesn't the straight media give a more accurate impression of what is going on?

I agree that more stories could be run, more interest shown. But if you read the papers carefully, you can find reportage on gay lib events far more frequently than in years past. Most of the significant meetings or decisions *are* covered, and although a reporter is sometimes assigned to a gay story who hasn't much idea of what is happening, more reporters are assigned to such stories who are most perceptive, if not in total sympathy. Straight media is straight media is straight media: Reporters, subeditors, chief editors, all have jobs to keep, reputations to think of. Any strong homosexual bias ends up excised from their copy, or they end up excised from the media. It is lamentably the way things are.

And always will be?

No, I think progress is being made. The fact of the existence of *Straight Answers* is a witness to that. Plans for detailed articles on the gay movement are, I am informed, in the files, and will be run when the time is right.

When is that?

When some appropriate news event with homosexuality as its basis occurs. The trial of Sergeant Matlovitch stirred a good deal of consideration of homosexuality in the straight media (lead article in *Time*, much coverage elsewhere). The news event must be of a positive nature, as, indeed, Sergeant Matlovitch's trial was. I take it as a plus sign that these planned detailed considerations of the gay lib movement have *not* been released at the time of some negative homosexual news event, such as a murder or entrapment episode. I believe it is safe to say that there is little taste in the straight media or among straight people for further "knocking" of gay people, but, it appears, the moment for a true and creative consideration of gay life has not quite arrived. And then, there are hitches in the gay movement.

What hitches?

It is my feeling that the political lobbying of gay people, its dedication and at times fanaticism, has still got the cart before the horse.

How so?

Any legislative body represents, however raggedly, the opinion of its constituents. Constituents are citizens, people. Until more American people are convinced that gay is good and that gay life-styles are valid (besides being inevitable), I don't see how gay lobbyists can successfully sway legislatures to revoke anti-gay laws and replace those with pro-gay legislation. I believe that before any avalanche of legal favor toward gays can gain momentum, *a better climate of opinion in this country toward homosexuality has got to be established.*

I spoke to one gay libber whose integrity I do not question, but he seemed determined to "force" issues politically, and felt that only by force could corrective (gay) legislation be initiated, completed. He argued that gay lobbyists might not be able to get laws passed that would compel straight people to receive gay people into their homes, but that such laws could be passed that would compel straight people to offer equal opportunities to avowed gay people in most other areas. I don't know whether or not he is correct in his premise, but his premise is objectionable to me on the face of it. I think he will not succeed as long as legislative bodies, as I said, represent their constituents. Personally, an enlightened legislator might agree with gay lib aims, and once in a while such a person may be found who feels the courage of his convictions *do* represent the will of the majority of people who elected him, and he is able to act legitimately in voting for gay lib proposals. But he or she is a rarity. Many are convinced, I suspect, of the legitimacy of gay lib proposals but are not convinced in the least that their constituents feel the same thing; in fact, the opposite. I can't understand how gay lib lobbyists can imagine that force can influence such a legislator.

Now, it is true that both processes—lobbying and changing the climate of opinion—must go on simultaneously. But the hitch in the gay lib movement (as I conceive it) is this: Far too few literate (not literary) people are out-and-out devoted to changing public opinion, and far too many are involved in the showy activities of the gay political arena.

What is meant by "showy"?

Bluntly, it's relatively easy to develop a political stance; it's not so easy to become a real human being who happens to be homosexual. The political arena offers a certain kind of notoriety, and even a minimal financial reward, while the quiet task of living an open and valid life as a homosexual offers little obvious reward, though much inner reward. I regret to say that gay movement activists seem to me psychologically suspect, more often than not. They have found a method of achieving a "name" in the world, and they are too often intoxicated with that, and exploitive of it, and highly incensed when their "authority" as an old hand is not recognized, or impinged upon by other "authorities" lately arrived in the movement, whom they set upon as interlopers. Bad business—the infighting. All the self-canonizers who "were there first," who indeed fought some of the early battles of gay lib, and who will never let others forget it—are undoing all their good work with this kind of overweening pride. And then, these political, gay lib old hands tend to become increasingly fanatic—or gay lib dropouts when the going gets tough. As fanatics, they are an unruly bunch, and they lose sight of reasonable ways and means to achieve their aims, and become far more interested in perpetuating their personal "fame" than in representing gay people. *Their* "constituents" are left far behind, a fact that David Goodstein has underscored, to his credit. In composing his national lobby, he weeded out gay libbers with a tendency to opportunize their personal position, and chose gay libbers who are interested in the issues and capable of getting things done, quietly. He separated the men from the boys (difficult to do for gay people, I admit), the self-aggrandizers and neurotics, from the dedicated and effective gay individuals.

This squabbling, infighting, reaches the ken of the straight media, and it causes that media, I feel, to hesitate to proffer full treatment.

Now, now, for my gay readers—let me reaffirm my belief in gay lib—but let me remind you that the kids at the Stonewall Bar the night of the raid were not wise-ass politicos, they were just the usual kids in a dance bar. As I remember the bar, with its encaged go-go boys and two dance floors, it was patronized by ribbon clerks (me) and by working kids in all the professions and services. They reacted to suppression, they gave voice for the first time en masse to gay lib aims. It is a breaking of faith with them to misrepresent them now with certain ongoing gay lib practices. They were not fanatics or proselytizers or especially badly dressed; they were just kids dancing in an ordinary gay bar who wanted something gay people have never had: inclusion as citizens in the rights granted by the Bill of Rights. They were not, as some of our present gay lib people are, theatrically willful in their protest, or specialized as barbed speakers, or protective of some inane territory of authority or precedence. They were gay people, young mostly, who were *hurt,* as surely as the young people at Kent State were hurt, and killed—and it was that bullying and their hurt to which good people in America responded with concern. It is that hurt that subsequent gay lib leaders might keep in mind when political infighting begins, or when personal pride supersedes other motives.

Incidentally, the human temptation to posit oneself as a wise-ass politico in the gay movement has unpleasant reverberations in the minds of gay people old enough to remember the communist movements of the 1930s. I am amazed and appalled at how much of the technical-political lingo-of-organization gay libbers have picked up: "caucus," "movement," "cell," and just general outlook as "professional" gay libbers. Awful.

It's relatively easy and alas possible to become politically inspired, to invest the gay lib cause with energy that had better be applied to living an exemplary human existence as a homosexual. It amuses me when a vociferous gay libber finds oppression everywhere, when his attention is devoted exclusively to proselytizing, defending his position in arcane procedural arguments—but he admits not having the courage to bend to the task of telling his parents he's gay, which, if everyone like him proceeded to do, would accomplish far more for gay lib than his most strenuous abstract efforts. He has become hooked on a *cause;* obsessed with the right things, but for wrong reasons. I find crusty, professional been-through-it-all gay libbers not only boring but obstacles to implementing the aims of gay lib.

Are there gay communists?

I have been at meetings of the Gay Academic Union where a *socialist* held the floor—are they dull!—and he rattled off all the cliches you have ever heard: I thought that stuff died or fell apart like old Essex cars. Not on your life: just as routine a spiel as we used to hear, nothing new added. I am all for giving everybody a voice—and gay people at their meetings having been suppressed so many years bend over backward to do that—but socialists (and women using what they call disruptive dyke tactics) ought to be . . . well, put on a stopwatch. No, I haven't been aware of any "party infiltration" as the "commies" used to call it. Gay people have only to check the records: Communism, fascism, and nazism didn't give homosexuals any place in their societies except a fast cattle car to the concentration camps.

180

What is a "zap"?

A militant and dramatic method gay libbers of five or six years ago used to *crash* certain establishment citadels where they were denied a hearing, or even entry. Walter Cronkite got it in his inner sanctum, CBS studio.

Did zapping work?

It got attention, and zapping was needed then. I think gay lib has arrested attention, now gay practitioners (of zaps) get arrested.

Do gay people like to think of themselves as a persecuted minority, on a par with Jews, blacks, Italians, etc.?

I don't imagine any group "likes" to think of themselves that way. It seems certain gay groups have so characterized themselves; they are precisely correct in that they *have been persecuted* for the fact of their homosexuality. But there is so much cross-cutting of social and ethnic lines by homosexuals that for me the comparison with clear-cut minorities has no point. Gay is black, Jewish, Italian, etc. I think homosexuals have banded together and are fighting and hope to receive recognition and fair treatment as a group, but somehow the classification of gay people as a minority, to be treated as such, isn't enough. To put it mildly.

Do gay people believe that one day in America their relationships will be considered by society on a par with heterosexual relationships?

Yes. As Christopher Isherwood stated in his seminar at the Modern Language Association convention a couple of years ago, there'll come a day in this country when homosexuality will be "a perfectly natural thing."

What about those gay lib prophets who predict the unisex-ing of the whole world?

A shade futuristic for me, but a possibility, I suppose. I do not believe I will be around to see it, nor will many others, nor, frankly, would I want to. I like the whole thing as it is, and do believe the job at hand as articulated by Mr. Isherwood is our first commitment.

Is there an active organization called Parents for Gays?

Yes, would that it had a chapter in every city! What consternation and heartbreak among parents this organization has prevented. I read a description of one of their meetings: A new couple (parents) come to a gathering—having been tricked or clubbed or blackmailed into attendance usually. They stand in a corner and hate the other parents of gays, and then they are drawn into a little conversation about their son and his homosexuality, and they listen to other parents talking knowledgeably and proudly about their gay sons and daughters, and the new couple sees that other parents have "found out" and survived, and they begin to understand that maybe their world and their relationship with their gay son hasn't ended forever, and they even glimpse the thing they could hardly have ever conceived: their acceptance for the boy as he is, and their good thoughts that *he* has found the sexual adjustment that is right for him, that will make *him* happy. This is the customary evolution in the thinking and feeling of new parent-members; it takes a while, the article says, but it *takes*, and families stay together and love triumphs, which is the way I like it.

What is the National Gay Task Force?

One of the most effective ongoing organizations gay people have to represent them. I urge you to look up the phone number of the branch in your city, or the nearest city, and request every single piece of literature they have available. You will discover their aims, their accomplishments, and their present preoccupations. You can subscribe to their newsletter, which will keep you up-to-date. The National Gay Task Force numbers among its members people I consider effective gay lib leaders. You don't hear much about the NGTF, I don't, but it comforts me to know that it exists. If I were a joiner, and I am not, I would join it. I regret to say gay lib organizations have come and gone, including some of the early ones which helped a lot, but NGTF continues. The little dogs bark, but *that* caravan moves on.

Is it true that gay libbers and women's lib people have a hard time getting along?

Yes, there seems to be friction. When gay men and women settle down to the routine of being organized—difficult for sensitized and sensitive people—I think that friction will abate. The ideas both groups are trying to implement are new in human experience, at least in this country, and I find that *I* am uncomfortable in a meeting where gay lib and women's lib confront each other. A sort of carping attitude is liable to overcome one. Anyone. It seems a compulsion of both gay men and women when they get together: a nagging disapproval on both sides. Perhaps if that attitude were recognized, it could be dealt with in a positive way. I have some idea how it originates, but that's not important; it is important to admit this carping attitude exists, and that like other gay lib obstacles, it has to be overcome, and it will be. Amazing to me how in relatively small groups of gay men and women or on a one-to-one basis, there is less disapproval or none. But en masse too often, one mess.

Ideally, what can each and every gay person do to facilitate faster pro-gay legislation?

I've said it before: If each and every gay person turned to his parents and said, I am gay, you'd be surprised how fast progay legislation would be passed. I realize that such a declaration is difficult or impossible for many gays, but *ideally*—ooo-woof—how late the lights would burn in the lairs of the lawmakers!

183

Should gay mothers and fathers be allowed to keep their children?

At ages one through five, did *you* know what the hell your mother or father did in bed? And after that, did you care? Would you renounce your parents, one or both, for being gay? I must say the only point of view that's worth consideration is the point of view of the child about to be deprived (by a judge) of its parents! I've never heard of or met a gay mother or father who wasn't proud as punch of his child or children, and who didn't do a conscious and conscientious job of raising children. Case closed.

Is there actually gay-lib-sponsored literature for teen-agers dealing with gay romance?

The American Library Association selects and places information and stories about young gay people and gay love in its proper place in libraries. I wish, in my early teens, I could have come across and read just *one* such story! What years of alienation, of feeling I was the only one, might have been salvaged. The teens, indeed, are when most gay people experience the powerful and particular homosexual urge within, so what better time for confirming through selected and well-written literature the fact that one is not alone.

Isn't there a danger of suggesting to children of an impressionable age a way of life, homosexual, which is undesirable?

What ever happened to those "children of an impressionable age"? I haven't heard about them in a long time, delightful! I suspect these days such children, if extant, watch TV programs; they scream with laughter at Wayland Flowers' witty puppet, Madame (a raunchy dowager type); they exult in violence to life and property with their favorite detective killers and maimers; they have seen childbirth live; they have witnessed social skulduggery in British and American house-

184

holds; they are expert on the vicious feeding habits of shark, cobra, and scorpion. Is there a single child left who, when he goes to the library and is old enough to read, retains innocent impressionability . . . to the point where he might be shocked by homosexuality! I recall the story of a friend of mine of *un*impressionable age, who decided to tell his younger, teen-age brother he was gay. They sat in a secluded place in the house, and my friend "confessed," with the remark to begin with that his confession might seem strange (to the younger boy). "Oh, listen, babe," the younger boy said matter-of-factly. "You're upset over nothing. I've had a lover in junior high school for two years. He's the captain of the hockey team." Now I don't imagine that all junior high school kids are quite that liberated—but not far from it. I suspect that by the time these kids of supposedly impressionable age get around to the gay stuff in the library, they've already seen a gay porn flick and will consider the reading material pretty tame.

Can there be a future in government for declared gay people?

Yes. Probably not as President, but that's a thankless job anyway. A number of legislators around the country have "come out," and it hasn't affected their standing with their constituents. Elaine Noble of Massachusetts is an example. There has always been room in the State Department for gay people. They're effective in positions where tact is essential, and they are notable peacemakers. For more information, inquire of the National Gay Task Force and I'm certain they can supply you with a list of "declared" gay legislators, and people active in other branches of government. The charge that gay federal employees are subject to blackmail has long ago been disproved. Harry Truman retained among his closest working associates several who were known homosexuals, bless Harry. Incidentally, Harry Truman's resurgent posthumous popularity is in large measure due to the dedicated interest of another "declared" homosexual, Merle Miller, whose book about Truman, *Plain Speaking*, topped the best-seller list for months and was adapted for TV.

Gay activity is against the law in most states. Do you advocate breaking the law?

The words of two great men come to mind in answer to your question. I feel about *laws* regulating my sex life the way Winston Churchill felt about "small countries": If they don't bother me, I won't bother them. Second, the words of Henry David Thoreau in his essay on civil disobedience: He urged us to break the law if we disbelieved in it, but to be prepared for the consequences of the test. If it should happen that I am arrested in some state that enforces laws against the sexual activity of consenting adults in private, I am psychologically ready to take the immediate consequences, and sufficiently knowledgeable to know how to legally defend myself, and make of my case a test of the law. I will not go out of my way to cause this to happen, nor will I avoid gay sexual activity in states that prohibit it. But if it comes, I shall stand with Thoreau, and fight.

Do you really contend that the Bill of Rights extends to homosexuals in terms of homosexual sex activity?

I do. The Bill of Rights and the Declaration of Independence apply to all American citizens and as long as a homosexual is an American he is entitled to be included under every proviso. I feel there is actually one section especially suited to the needs of homosexuals, and I am thinking of the phrase that guarantees to all citizens the right of "pursuit of happiness." Those old boys knew their onions, I mean the founding fathers. They included that phrase, it seems to me, not with gay people in mind, but as an open-ended "right" to cover exigencies they knew they could not foresee, human nature being as various and unpredictable as it is. Such an exigency has arisen in the needs of gay people to pursue happiness in their own way. It is my belief that as long as my pursuit of happiness as a homosexual does not in any way interfere with your pursuit of happiness, I am entitled under the Bill of Rights to pursue that happiness and do what I please with a consenting adult in private. I cannot think of a clearer or more pointed application of my right to happiness. I wish gay people in defense of themselves would make greater use of that guarantee.

Your Homosexual Sensibility

In *Straight Answers*, you have gained a revised and more understanding attitude toward a homosexual when he walks into a room where you are.

Second, you have come to grasp the fact that the homosexual sensibility hinges on love, not power.

Third, you have realized that homosexuals are not creatures from another planet, that they are people with the same emotional range as yourself.

Fourth, you have identified the possibility of a homosexual impulse in yourself, with its concomitant emphasis on love, as an ameliorating force to the heterosexual power drive, and as a key to the reality of your own unconscious mind.

I have told you something of myself, and you are aware that it is no more of a problem, and no cause for a muscle-spasm, to get to know people who are homosexual than it has been to know me.

You have learned that gay people are under fire, and what may seem to you off-putting about them are the defenses against fear that gay people raise. No, gay people are not better than straight people, just different, and no, gay people do not want to take over the world, they just want the right to live their own lives in peace and in harmony with everyone else. That harmony consists in loving as they choose and in making and being rewarded for their work contributions to the society in which we live.

It is my belief that you will derive a personal benefit from what you have learned in *Straight Answers*. Should a relative, friend, or business associate come to you with an admission of homosexuality, you are in a position to care for and counsel him.

You are also in a position to recognize and properly care for aspects in your own psyche of a "shadow-side," containing a homosexual potential, which exists in all of us, and which can be in you a matrix of love, depending upon the attitude you take toward it. I hope I have shown you how to appreciate it rather than deprecate it, and what a source of the "treasure hard to attain" that shadow-side can be. For me, it holds whatever I have experienced of a transcendent soul.

I have misgivings. When I look over the hard, glittering, busy, bartering world, I wonder if I have made gay people and gay problems significant to you, if I have really helped you to initiate your homosexual sensibility. Have I effectively eliminated the clutter of a tradition of revilement toward homosexuality that might deflect you in your discovery and consideration of that sensibility? I have tried, and that alone has been worth it to me. If you are set on a thinking and feeling course about homosexuality, rather than responding to fear and superstition concerning it; if you are receptive now as you were rejecting then, that much more of a conscious and perceptive life is available to you, a thing that has benefit in it.

Living beings are innately idiosyncratic. It is an act of high courage to fling in the face of life the absolute affirmation of all that constitutes the individual, nothing withheld. Gay people have only recently mustered this courage-to-be, declaring what is vulnerable about themselves and everything that is unique. In so doing, they have become participants in the mystic drama of self-realization: united within, and in touch in themselves with a secret heart of love. I know you have lived this drama, too. May we begin to live it together?